The Last of the Cavaliers

Steve Smith Eccles
with Alan Lee

PELHAM BOOKS
LONDON

PELHAM BOOKS

Published by the Penguin Group
27 Wrights Lane, London W8 5TZ
Viking Penguin Inc.,
375 Hudson Street, New York, New York 10014, USA
Penguin Books Australia Ltd, Ringwood, Victoria, Australia
Penguin Books Canada Ltd,
10 Alcorn Avenue, Toronto, Ontario, Canada M4V 3B2
Penguin Books (NZ) Ltd,
182–190 Wairau Road, Auckland 10, New Zealand

Penguin Books Ltd, Registered Offices: Harmondsworth, Middlesex,
England

First published in Great Britain 1993

Copyright © Steve Smith Eccles with Alan Lee 1993

Typeset in Monophoto 11$\frac{1}{2}$ on 13pt Sabon by
Selwood Systems, Midsomer Norton, Avon
Printed in Great Britain
by Butler & Tanner Ltd, Frome and London

A CIP catalogue record for this book is available from the
British Library

ISBN 0 7207 1887 2

The moral right of the author has been asserted

The Last of the Cavaliers

Contents

Illustrations

Chapter One

'His only effort appears to be aimed at being a nuisance; when present. A pity, as he has some ability.'

'He does very little work even when he is in school. His classroom behaviour is far from perfect.'

'He still sees his role in life as someone who must attract attention by frivolous disruption of order.'

'Have seen very little of him this term.'

'He is a capable boy who, if he would stop trying to be the James Cagney of Swanwick, would do very well.'

Comments from the final school report of Steve Smith Eccles, July 1970.

The great mystery, looking back on it, is how I ever came to like horses at all. The first three I came across, in a childhood far removed from thoroughbreds in every sense, were the horse which pulled the grocer's cart, a pony belonging to a girl in the village, and a pit pony. I was scared rigid by the first, bitten by the second and kicked by the third. Why I did not give up all crazy ideas about a career in racing, there and then, I cannot imagine.

My home village was Pinxton, which straddles the border between Nottinghamshire and Derbyshire and, in those days, was almost exclusively a mining community. We lived in Kirkstead Rows, a development of mining cottages which at least had symmetry in its favour. The cottages, all two-up, two-down, were built back to back. There were four rows, with unmade roads dividing the frontages. Drury the grocer trundled up and down the rows a couple of days each week with his horse and cart, carrying food supplies and almost every other essential for the house-tied womenfolk. It was probably a gentle old horse but, to an impressionable half-pint like me, there was something alarming about his size and his relentless clip-clopping plod. I ran to hide whenever I heard him coming.

I was a little older when I showed a fateful interest in that girl's pony – or, if the truth be told, in the girl. Maybe this was the first stirring of sexuality in the young Eccles, though oddly I cannot recall the girl's name, but I have no trouble with the pony. Its name was Amber and when, in offering it food to show off in front of the girl, I was bitten more viciously than playfully, I was packed off to the doctor's for a tetanus jab. It might, I suppose, have turned me off both horses and girls. But it didn't.

And then came the pit pony. Any who mistakenly believe a racehorse has an uncomfortable life might like to compare the constant pampering and affection within a racing stable with the existence of these wretched creatures. As a teenager, my Dad had been responsible for looking after the pit ponies at our local colliery. For fifty weeks of each year, they lived underground, stabled in pretty basic style at the foot of the shaft and working, on shifts similar to the men, pulling the loaded railway trucks. They had two weeks' 'holiday' each year and would emerge, blinking pathetically in the unaccustomed light.

Small wonder that the ponies shared a fiery and distrustful nature. When they came up for air each summer, the lads of the village would parade their macho skills by trying to ride them bareback. It was a pretty unsatisfactory rodeo, five seconds being standard time for staying on board, and when I joined in this dubious sport, I was unceremoniously kicked by a particularly resentful pony. In retrospect, I can't say I blame him.

I did not need this tender dissuader to convince me that there were better things in life than going down the pit each day. That, I think, had been one of the earliest and most irreversible decisions of my life.

My grandfather apparently helped sink the shaft at Langton Colliery and, whether to show me my future or to warn me of a life to avoid, Dad took me down there. In that frightening hour underground, I knew I would be breaking the family tradition. I suppose the majority of my parents' generation had little choice in the matter; they were born into mining and expected to do as everyone else in the community did. But I had a choice and I made it that day, having experienced claustrophobia for the first time in my young life and not enjoyed it one bit.

Dad always said there was decent money to be made down the pit if you were prepared to work at it, and I don't doubt he was right. Each miner was given a 'stint', a yardage of coal to get out, and the good workers might do two 'stints' in a shift. But it was the conditions which appalled me, the need to crawl on your belly for several hundred yards just to get to the coal face, then to balance on your knees, swinging your pick in a very confined space.

The grubby side of the job did not deter me and neither did the raw material. I grew up with coal and I loved it. Mum despaired of the times she would find me in the coalhouse, sucking a piece of the stuff. When I grew older, my mates and I would play war games on the ash tips, which were warm all the year round. And we swam, even in midwinter, in the water at the foot of the slagheap. It was called Pookey's Brook and it never froze, but its water was black and it felt like swimming in treacle. We used old tin tubs as navy boats and created our fantasy land from an area which would now be thought hideous.

Videos and Space Invader machines were still unheard of, so the kids of my generation spent their time in the great outdoors and I, for one, loved the feeling of space and freedom. It was not, though, a luxurious upbringing. Nowadays it would be thought extremely basic. Yet we had everything we needed and memory tells me I was happy. Ours was a large family, in the custom of the day. Mum was the eldest of eleven, while my Dad had two brothers and four sisters. His side of the family would have been considerably bigger but three sets of twins died at, or soon after birth. My generation was much more manageable; it was just me and my sister.

June 9 1955 was the day when the Eck came into the world, a son for Stanley and Joan and another burden for my grandmother, not that she seemed to mind. We all lived in granny's cottage in the early days and she spoiled me rotten. There was not enough space for me to have a separate room and I would sleep propped up between Mum and Dad in their bed. I'm told I was a bit of a cry-baby and I have a curiously vivid memory of being given a piece of liver, one day, to stop me howling. I played with this liver as if it was a lump of plasticine, rolling it around the floor among the dust and doghairs. Then it was taken away from me, washed, cooked and served up for my Uncle Ian's dinner when he came back from the pit. Quite why that has stuck in my mind I don't know but I suppose it is an example of how nothing was allowed to go to waste in our home!

Dad went to the pit each morning with his sandwiches in a metal box. We called it a snap tin, 'snap' being the colloquial for food round our way, and when he came home again at night I would always grab the tin and try to wrestle the lid off. I never did manage it, but I knew there would, without fail, be a bar of Milky Way inside for me, Dad's daily present from the canteen. On Fridays, as well as the chocolate, there would be a threepenny bit as pocket-money.

I always made it go a long way. Even in those infant years, the entrepreneurial spirit was growing in me and I would look to earn extra by doing errands and generally making myself popular. If I was not short of initiative, however, I think I lacked something in bravery as a small boy. The grocer's horse was not the only terror of my impressionable life. I was also scared of the dark, which did not sit comfortably with the fact that we had an outside loo. This needs explaining. Our loo was actually across the road, adjoining the coalhouse and backing onto the cottage in the next row. It had no lighting and, even in the middle of the day, I found it eerie. So I would sit on the loo with the door wide open, looking out at, and fully observed by, anyone strolling past down the road.

Starting junior school was no great adventure for me. Kirkstead Row school was literally at the bottom of the garden, convenient in one sense but something of a handicap when it came to skiving. I used to leave the house, walk down the short garden, feed our chickens at the bottom, then hop over the fence into school. Our class teacher's name was Miss Freeman and I still have a battered old photograph showing her in long-suffering pose, presiding over a distinctly mixed bunch of angelic little girls and boys who might have come straight from the pages of *Just William*. The young Smith Eccles is not exactly a picture of sartorial elegance but the sight which still curls me up now is that of my best mate,

Piwi Inman, a scruffy young bruiser if ever there was one. I was bright enough at school and it held no terrors for me. Equally, it held no special pleasure and I longed for the holidays, the war games at Pookey's Brook and, each year, the two great adventures – a family holiday in Skegness and a few boyishly busy weeks with my cousins.

Skegness was an institution. When the pit closed down for its annual summer fortnight, Pinxton packed its bags and, en masse, boarded a steam train for the east coast. It may sound pretty unimaginative but that was the way things were done. Saturday morning, we arrived at the station and found all our neighbours on the platform. The train pulled out and the young heads sticking out of the windows were schoolmates who were now going to share their holidays, too.

One year, we rebelled against this and went to Cornwall instead. But it didn't seem quite the same. We were back at Skeggie the next year. We always stayed on a caravan site called Ingermills and the routine was such that, if I went back to Skegness now, I reckon I could still walk round the town blindfold. There were donkeys on the beach, which gave me an early introduction to slow conveyances, but the highlight for me was always accompanying the caravan site foreman, Bill, when he went around on his tractor emptying the bins.

This was just about my ideal. I was active, on the move, meeting people and doing something which involved a bit of strength, a bit of showing off. The extrovert tendencies were there, even as an infant, but, because I was pretty small, they could sometimes land me in trouble. One such occasion was when I fell through the ice of a frozen pond and had my life saved by my cousin, Graham.

Graham was one of Auntie Doris's five kids. Doris was Dad's sister and she had her work cut out in more than simply numerical ways. Her two first-borns were girls but the three boys who followed were all deaf and dumb. There was Mike, Graham and John and, as I grew up with them, I learned to communicate by using their sign language. Even now, it is the only other language I have mastered.

Graham was the same age as me and it seemed natural that we should be close. He was family but he was also one of my best pals. I don't think it ever occurred to either of us to feel,

Who's a pretty boy, then!

Smith Eccles's first ride in public.

much less show, any self-consciousness about his disability. Once we had devised our means of making each other understood, I never so much as gave it a thought.

Physically, though, we were very different boys. Graham was big and excessively strong. He had enormous hands and, even as a young boy, he was a natural grafter. This suited me fine and when Graham, aged a mere eight, got a job labouring on a local farm for a man called Nash, I followed suit, earning sixpence a week for doing odd jobs there in my holidays.

It was, in truth, not so much a farm as a smallholding, and a pretty ramshackle one at that. But old Nash was a versatile soul and he did not mind what he asked us to do. One of his duties, for instance, was to tend the local graveyard and, one summer, he had Graham and me digging graves. They had to be carefully dug to the regulation six-foot depth and, as the soil was clay, it was backbreaking work for a couple of junior-schoolboys. I think it must have been in those weeks that I developed the arm muscles which have served me well in later life.

We made our killing at potato-picking time. They were hard days, involving a 5 a.m. start, cycling the four miles to the farm and then toiling in the potato fields until almost dusk. But it was worth half-a-crown a day to us, which seemed close to a fortune. It was here during the Christmas holidays one year that the young life of Smith Eccles almost met a watery end. For all his diverse earning power, it seemed that Mr Nash was a far from wealthy man, for he had no running water in the farmhouse. This meant that when the animals needed water it had to be drawn in buckets from the farm pond, usually quite a straightforward business but, on this particularly arctic day, complicated by the ice.

Graham and I had been detailed to fetch water for the cows. I was seven years old, unable to swim a stroke but also unable to identify danger when I saw it. Blithely, I marched out onto the frozen pond with my bucket, looking for the areas where the ice had still not closed across the water.

The inevitable duly occurred. I slipped, and the sudden shift of even my featherweight was enough to crack the ice. I fell through the surface and sank, in unspeakable terror, into the torture chamber beneath. If Graham had not been on hand, I would certainly have drowned. I would still have drowned if he

Mum and Dad on holiday at Skegness.

The Class of '59—Kirkstead Rows School. I'm the one on the left.

8

had not acted with such typical bravery and strength. I am told he swung his bucket over his head and smashed it down on the ice, making a big enough hole for him to dive through and pull me out.

We were not allowed in the farmhouse and we were unsure what the reaction of farmer Nash might be to this near-disaster, so we did not risk going to him for help. Instead, Graham built a fire in the orchard and I stood there shivering in my underpants while my other clothes were dried. I caught a chill, of course, but that was a small price to pay for coming out of such a scrape with my life. That day, I really did regret Graham's condition, for the words of gratitude I felt were left unspoken. Sometimes, sign language is not sufficient to express feelings.

The outdoor theme to my life was reflected in my hobbies. Sitting around at home with a good book or some music was not for me; it was to be much later before I learned to appreciate the therapeutic virtues of reading. No, I had to be out and doing, and I was only about nine when I developed a fascination for birdwatching.

This is still listed as my hobby in the *Directory of the Turf*, the who's who of racing. For some reason I cannot fathom, most people who know me think I must be referring to birds of a human form rather than birds of a feather. They are wrong. Ornithology remains an interest to this day; as a boy, I had the best egg collection in Pinxton and I was proud of it. To the pure birdwatcher, this may not go down too well. The thrill of the long wait and the unusual sighting is, of course, gratification enough for diehard ornithologists. I spent plenty of time watching and waiting, too, but it was not sufficient for the adventurous spirit. During the breeding season, I reckoned I climbed every tree within five miles of Kirkstead Rows, gathering an array of eggs which were the envy of my classroom peers.

I did cheat once. Outrageously. Our school had a museum, nothing grand and not especially well attended, but a museum none the less. I had noticed, on a rare visit, that one of the items gathering dust in there was an ostrich egg. So I pinched it, added it to my collection and swaggeringly told my agog mates that I had found it on a slagheap. For days afterwards, they were all combing the area in search of giant, exotic birds which had somehow strayed into a Derbyshire pit village. Sadly, what had been a pretty good gag came badly unstuck when Mum somehow found out the truth. My reward was a thick ear, a stern lecture and instructions to take the egg back where it belonged. My tail drooping between my quivering legs, I took it to the headmaster, and received a second dose of punishment.

I may not have been the most impeccably behaved child at Kirkstead Rows but I was plenty bright enough to get by. I passed the 11-plus exam with distinction and so, in unaccustomed smart uniform, well scrubbed and brushed by a mother prouder of me than she would ever show, I began life at grammar school.

Swanwick Hall school was seven miles from Pinxton, so it was an early start on the bus each day. It also inevitably meant making new friends, and losing touch with old ones. I saw much less of my junior-school mucker, Piwi Inman, and of my deaf-and-dumb cousins. My new gang comprised 'Tich', 'Ched' and 'Evo', more formally Richard Naylor, Philip Gorgon and Clive Evans.

If my progress, academically, was halting, it was not so much through lack of intelligence as lack of ambition. I picked things up very quickly but, instead of pushing on to stay ahead of the pack, I then habitually loafed around while the stragglers caught up. I suppose I had no respect for learning, which was a pity, but by then, although I had no set idea what I wanted to do with my life, I was pretty sure it would not involve too many educational qualifications.

School was certainly not the best time of my life but I have no memory of it being the worst, either. And, if the times I best enjoyed were those when I did not have an exercise book open in front of me, I don't suppose I was very different from the majority in that.

I played right-wing at football, and considered myself to be rather dashing, but I gave up the game in search of pocket money. School football matches were on Saturday mornings and Saturday became an earning day for me early in my teens. Tich's father had a private coal-delivery round and Tich and I were recruited to help. The hundredweight bags of coal helped those muscles along and the three pounds a week helped my savings. It also contrasted starkly with the five shillings a week I took home in my first racing job.

I never missed a chance to make a bob or two at school. In

fact I became known, to the flattery of my ego, as the Al Capone of Swanwick Hall. The very unboyish activity of Domestic Science provided one of my best little earners.

One afternoon each week was devoted to subjects which we regarded as escapism. But, for my mate Ched and me, the options were limited. The woodwork teacher didn't like us, and we definitely did not like art. I suppose we might have battled through in one or the other but for the fact that the Domestic Science teacher was gorgeous. My interest in the opposite sex was now aroused and this was the clinching factor.

Each week, we were told in advance what we would be making, and the idea was that we should bring the ingredients from home. Jam was a popular choice, so dear old Mum, doubtless a little bewildered over this sudden interest in such a womanly thing as cooking, would pack up the necessary fruit, sugar etc. It was some time before she became suspicious about the fact that I never brought home any evidence of my labours and, when the truth was out, the scales rose from her eyes about my cooking enthusiasm and she was not best pleased.

What I had done was to locate a few shops on the way home which would pay me a bob or two for my jars of jam. So, after each domestic science afternoon, I would come home with nothing to show off to my Mum but with coins chinking decadently in my trouser pocket.

The longer I stayed at school, the less attention I paid to my lessons. In the summer, if the weather was good, I did not even pay them the compliment of turning up, though for days on end I went through a charade which made the truancy seem more acceptable. I dressed in uniform, caught the bus at the appointed time and sometimes even used the journey to do the previous night's homework, cannily cribbed from some poor, industrious and intimidated lad. Once at school, I stood angelically at assembly and answered my name at the register check. Then, as the workers went off to their classes, I would slip quietly away and begin to walk home.

There were any number of stopping-off points but I would always make sure I arrived back in Pinxton at 4.30 p.m., synchronised with the school bus. Someone must have known how many lessons I was skipping but I don't think my Mum and Dad ever did.

You will notice, perhaps, that horse-racing has not merited so much as a mention in these childhood reminiscences. The reason for this is that I had no contact with horses, other than those previously mentioned, and my knowledge of racing was confined to the televised meetings on a Saturday afternoon, when Dad would have his ten bob each way and, utterly illogically, I would tell him earnestly that I was going to be a jockey.

I had heard that a boy from the next village had gone into racing and, without having the first idea what it involved, it began to gnaw away at me that this was the kind of life I wanted. Possibly, I was doing it by default, because I was intent on avoiding the pit and could not think of anything else to do. Certainly, I was doing it unconventionally. Most boys who come into racing have horses in their blood. Most have ridden ponies, some have excelled at showjumping. I had never had or ridden a pony and I had not so much as seen a racehorse. But my mind was made up and I shall always be grateful that Mum and Dad saw how determined I was and made no effort to dissuade me. Their support was to be important throughout, but here it was crucial.

Dad asked around and came up with a short-list of three trainers, then wrote to each of them, giving details of my age, height and weight, and asking if there was a vacancy for an apprentice. Arthur Stephenson in Bishop Auckland said he did not want apprentices, only stable-lads – a response for which I am now profoundly grateful. I am not sure gruff old Arthur, now sadly passed on, and I would have lasted long together. Frenchie Nicholson in Cheltenham, whose reputation was great in taking on teenagers and making them jockeys, turned me down because he said I was too heavy. This left Tom Jones. I knew no more of him than I did of the others and it was to be some time before I appreciated my good fortune in having him for a mentor. Doubtless, like most trainers answering such an inquiry, he saw in me no more than cheap labour. But he wrote back offering me a month's trial and, on 21 July 1970, feeling uncomfortably smart in a newly bought pinstripe suit, and clutching a battered old leather suitcase, I set off for Newmarket. It was the first time I ever saw my mother cry.

Chapter Two

Dear Mum, Dad and Diane,

Settling in quite well, but I wish I was at home. It's a bit rough getting up at 6 a.m. every morning including Sunday.

The meals aren't bad but I would sooner have yours, Mam. I have heard from the head lad, Mr Edgley, that I'm not allowed any time off in the first year if I pass my trial, not even at Christmas.

My first week's wages will be about £1 4s 3d (not much). I could earn that in one day coaling. 2s of the above I have to pay for the television room each week, plus 5s 6d down the laundrette.

I don't do much at the stable, only fill hay sacks, muck out, water the horses and feed the pigs.

The governor hasn't even spoken to me yet.

Love Steve

28 July 1970, Newmarket

[Text of my first letter home as a working lad.]

Harry Thomson Jones was an Army man, a cavalry officer in wartime, and it showed in the way he regimented his stable-yard. Everything at Green Lodge had to be spotless and shining; if it was not, there was hell to pay. The same could not be said for the first home, away from home, I had ever experienced. My digs were squalid and the combination of this and the intimidating new disciplines under my first real employer meant that I spent the first week of my life in racing fervently wishing myself back in the cosy community of the mining village. There were times,

I think, when I would even have gone down the pit to escape from this frightening purgatory for which I had so keenly volunteered.

Dad and Uncle Ian drove me to Newmarket. It was a Sunday, the quietest day of the week for a racing stable but still not entirely an idle one. Morning stables would just have finished when our car nosed into Newmarket High Street and, with only the address of the digs at our disposal, we stopped to ask directions from a lad on the pavement.

Now, I have become quite a believer in fate and coincidence and here is one good reason why. When we asked this kid if he could direct us to a number in Nat Flatman Street, he said that not only did he know where it was, he actually lived in the house himself and was heading there now. His name turned out to be Tommy Keddy and, for twenty years, he has been my best and closest friend.

Nat Flatman was apparently a jockey in bygone days, though the name meant nothing to me. His street was not especially attractive but, for generations, it has served a purpose for the youthful itinerants of the town's racing industry. Fred Winter once had digs in Nat Flatman Street and even I had heard of him.

We gave Tommy a lift and he told us to pull up at a corner house, opposite a fish-and-chip shop. It did not look palatial but appearances were deceptive. It was much worse than that.

My first landlady was known as Ma Coogan and, if you created the role model for sleazy backstreet landladies, she would come close to getting the part. I had only been there a few days when I came back to the house at lunchtime and found her in the kitchen making a stew. It was not a welcoming sight. Judged by the food she had served up to date, the stew would have been nothing worth looking forward to in any case, but as Ma stood over it, her hair unkempt and her glasses lending an unpleasant meanness to her face, a cigarette hung limply from her mouth. Ash fell from its end into the stew, with Ma Coogan showing not the slightest concern.

Her cooking was uniformly dreadful but we lads ate everything served up for the simple reason that we could afford nothing better. There was a strict ban on bringing food into the house but we did devise a plan to get around this. The fire escape from our room comprised a knotted rope with a three-pronged hook at its top end. We used to turn the rope upside down, lowering the hook to the street. One of us would have slipped across the road to the chip shop and the food, in its traditional newspaper wrapping, could then be attached to the hook and hauled up through the window for a bedroom feast.

In our case, this involved six lads. I don't quite know what I had expected, on day one at Ma Coogan's, but even in my worst-case scenario I had not envisaged sharing an ordinary-sized room with five other lads. There was enough room for three bunk beds and precious little else. Not for us the luxury of an armchair or two, nor even the functional desirables such as a table and chair for letter-writing. It was 'top bunk or bottom' and be thankful for small mercies. I later discovered that Dad was so appalled by our first sight of the digs on that July Sunday that he was reluctant to leave me. For a few days, I very much wished he had not. I cried myself to sleep for the first few nights and the working routine, although immediately fascinating to me, was so new, disciplined and arduous that I seriously doubted whether I could stick at it.

On my first Monday morning I reported to the guv'nor at 6.30 a.m. sharp. Punctuality, I was to learn, rated high among Tom Jones's priorities, as did smartness and hard work. If you fell short of his standards in any way, he did not mess around with quiet reminders. H.T. Jones was a hard taskmaster and if he did not throw his cap at a miscreant he would probably whack him with his swagger stick. We did not resent this. It was a discipline which was accepted. But the military style in which he ran his yard would not find such tolerance nowadays. He would have a revolt on his hands.

I felt nervous and conspicuous on that first day, cowed by the unfamiliar which surrounded me and uncomfortably aware that I was not properly dressed. I had no jodhpurs and no riding boots. Instead, I wore my old jeans and a serviceable pair of sneakers. Tom Jones had made it plain he would not accept this situation for long.

I was one of four new apprentices starting work at the yard. There was Peter Green, Paul Booth and a lad I remember only as 'Taffy'. I had feared that my inexperience would be as obvious as my old jeans but, to my surprise, the other three had never ridden before, either. We were all on a month's trial and we were all to survive that and stay, but we had to be doing it for our dreams because, at first, we were merely slave labour. The yard paid for our digs but we each took home less than £1 a week, which came pretty hard to me as I had been making a good deal more while at school.

We were given only the most menial jobs for a few days, sweeping the yard and feeding the stable pigs. Then, we were each assigned to one of the permanent, paid lads and, very gradually, given greater responsibilities.

A little old Irishman named Christy O'Connor was put in charge of me and, inside a fortnight, he had taught me many of the tricks of the trade. Christy was a master at cutting corners, at giving the pretence of hard work and efficiency when in reality he was bone idle. It was an art, though, I must grant him that.

Tom Jones insisted that his horses were strapped over twice each day. Christy's two horses always looked magnificent, glowing with health, yet to the best of my knowledge he never did any strapping at all. I found out after a while that his secret formula was linseed oil. He used to rub them down with the stuff because he knew it put a realistic if entirely artificial shine on their coats. Then he would sit in the corner of a box, hidden by a horse, smoking contentedly while giving a passable impression of the noise of a brush and comb. Anyone walking past the closed door of the box would assume that Christy was hard at work on his strapping.

The discipline of the yard extended to the daily polishing of head collars, cleaning of tools and sweeping and disinfecting of all the boxes during evening stables. But Christy never took any muck out at all. He found a way of burying it in the corner of his box, on the basis that one should never do anything today if it can be put off until tomorrow. He might not have been the best of influences for me but I liked the old fellow a lot. I also got along well with the other lads at the digs and, once the most acute of the homesickness had receded and my letters home became less frequent and less plaintive, I settled happily enough into the regulated lifestyle of a racing stable and began to develop the fanciful aspirations common to all would-be jockeys. I was to have a long wait for fulfilment.

Basically, we worked seven days a week, although one weekend in three would be off. Work began soon after six each morning, mucking out and tacking up the horses for exercise, which pulled out at 6.45. Breakfast followed and there was a rota among the apprentices for the job of running the half-mile into town to collect a consignment of bacon sandwiches and egg rolls for the lads. After that, the mucking-out and tacking-up procedure was repeated twice more, as we usually had three lots as against the two of most Newmarket yards at the time. Any idle moments were rapidly filled by orders to sweep up the yard or pull up weeds. H.T. Jones did not like to think any of his staff had nothing to do.

It was a standing joke in Newmarket that ours was always the last yard to finish the morning work and break for lunch. We consoled ourselves with the pious conviction that we did the job better than any of the opposition; in many ways, I think that was true. Tom's yard certainly had a deserved reputation, which meant that anyone who had served time with him carried with them a recommendation money could not buy, and would usually be at the front of the queue for any job in racing.

The apprentices had to report back at four o'clock each afternoon to clean and polish headcollars before the evening feed. Then we had to spend twenty minutes strapping each of our two horses before, at 6 p.m. precisely, the guv'nor appeared, stick under his arm, back erect, for his tour of inspection. We would stand nervously by our horses, saying nothing but praying that Tom would find nothing to rile him. He was strict and demanding, but scrupulously fair – though, on the odd occasion he was late for his walk round, it invariably meant he had had a drink or two at the races and so we waited in still greater trepidation for his judgements.

Tom Jones is in his late sixties now but remains one of the leading flat-race trainers in Newmarket. When I started out with him, however, he was predominantly a jumping man. Of the forty-plus horses in the yard, all but a dozen would be jumpers, but it was as well for us youngsters that he did keep a few flat horses as they were a more manageable size for us to ride.

First, though, we had to persuade the boss that we were capable and deserving of the job, and this was not done in a hurry. It was a feature of my apprenticeship that Tom brought me along at a pace he alone dictated. It was never fast enough for my liking, and there were times when frustration got the better of me. It is only at this distance that I can appreciate the worth of his methods.

The first horse I was allowed to ride was the stable-hack, an old thing called Battleonious. I can remember how self-conscious I felt as I was thrown up on him and told to walk him round a paddock, under critical eyes. After a few circuits I was instructed to make the hack trot. Part of me wishes this scene had been videoed; another part knows how I would squirm with embarrassment if ever I had to watch it. I had no idea how to make a horse trot by bumping the saddle and my initial efforts must have been laughable. After an hour of red-faced effort, I got the timing right and wondered how it could ever have seemed so difficult. I always have been one who wants to run before he can walk and I was now confident I was ready to ride any of the horses in their galloping work. The guv'nor was more realistic.

There were another few days of walking and trotting amid rising impatience before Tom decided I could be let loose on Newmarket Heath. From then on, each new step was like an exhilarating gear-change in a powerful car. At first, I was still on Battleonious and still only trotting – in truth, the poor old thing could barely have gone faster than a trot if I had asked him. Then, at last, I was allowed on a proper racehorse for a canter. Looking back now, we can't have been going any great pace but it was comfortably the fastest I had ever been and it was a sensation I shall never forget. That day, I was hooked. Any doubts I may have had were banished in those few breathtaking minutes meeting the wind in my face and sensing the ground rushing past beneath this great, beautiful beast. There was, quite suddenly, no way I could ever consider doing anything else.

It was two months before I had my first gallop. Five furlongs on a very moderate horse. To me, it was like a ride in Nigel Mansell's Formula One car. The surge of adrenalin was something I had not experienced before and the effect of riding at speed was a drug. I could not get enough, simply could not wait for the next 'fix'. The work-riding was my motivation and my bonus but the daily grind of the yard waited for no one. I had my two horses to look after and Tom was very adept at bringing me down to earth by forcefully pointing out a brass that was not shining as it should be. He knew how impetuous I was and he had his ways of controlling me. I believe it is well nigh impossible to be in the environment of a stable-yard without developing a genuine love of horses. Most people probably bring such a love with them but I had started from scratch, knowing nothing about the animals I was to work with. Nevertheless, it did not take long. The first horse I 'did' was Catherine Rose. She was next to useless at her job and would have needed quite a start to have won a race, but I thought she was gorgeous and grew very attached to her, so that when she left the yard, broken down I fear, I was more than fleetingly sad. In my five years at Tom's, I saw many lads in tears when they lost a horse and, if it never quite took me that way, I still had feelings.

The best horse I did was probably Noon, who won four novice chases one winter and kept winning races for some seasons. But there were many good horses in the yard and, like a class of schoolchildren, they all had their foibles and all needed treating as individuals.

The most evil of racehorses will usually develop a special affinity with their lads. Anyone else trying to enter the horse's box will be treated as an enemy and rudely ejected by any available means, yet these creatures can be like putty in the hands of that one special person who gives them feed and water and makes them look smart. Three such horses in our yard were Frozen Alive, Gorston Verran and Brushwood.

Frozen Alive had such a violent streak that a specially padded box had to be made for him. Like so many of his ilk, though, he had great ability and was one of the top novice hurdlers of his year. But he had no respect for authority, as he showed at evening stables one evening. It is a trainer's custom to feel his horses' legs at night, a custom that is habitually carried out in dread of feeling heat from some knock or strain, inevitably putting plans on hold. This particular evening, the guv'nor was in with Frozen Alive, whose head was being held in the usual way by his lad. As Tom picked up one of his legs, the horse flew into a fury, whipping round and, as the lad's grip on the lead-rein failed him, literally tearing Tom's shirt off his back.

Gorston Verran was just as evil, yet would behave with complete tranquillity for his lad, Joe Weatherall. This was a mite surprising as Joe was a formidable drinker and would stagger into his horse's box each evening, immune to his own fear and the horse's feelings. Gorston Verran would meekly allow old Joe to push and shove him around, yet any other, peaceable party would not be allowed near him. Whenever Joe had a weekend off, we all used to draw lots for the dubious pleasures of looking after his horse.

A fellow called Jack had a similar relationship with Brushwood, a regular schizophrenic of a horse. He was a big, bold grey, a decent jumper but a horrible character. Jack loved him, though, and somehow the feeling seemed to be mutual, until one awful evening when a vet came to take a blood sample. I was in the next box, strapping one of my own horses, and the vet was briefly alone with Brushwood. What he did to him I have no idea but the horse went berserk. Jack rushed in too late to calm him. The vet was trapped in one corner but, as Brushwood reared up and repeatedly kicked out, it was poor old Jack who took the full impact. Hearing this commotion, I left my horse and hurried out. Jack was lying in the straw with the love of his life trampling him mercilessly. He was dead when the ambulance arrived, the first corpse I had ever seen and, I would like to think, the last.

Stable-yards exist on a rollercoaster of triumph and tragedy but the joys and sorrows are customarily linked to the relative trivia of a horse's performance or, at worst, a horse's health. A man's death in our midst was something very different and, for days afterwards, a sombre mood descended on the place.

Eventually, life had to resume as before, our private incentives for being in this curious lifestyle driving away the demons which that incident had summoned to our workplace. I got on with my persistent hassling of Tom Jones, for, although I had never lost the sense of awed respect he instilled in all his young charges, I was intent on letting him know that I would stop at nothing to achieve my goal of race-riding. All too many apprentices fall by the wayside but I was determined to avoid all the pitfalls and quite happy to work my socks off in pursuit of the life I wanted. This open, sometimes vocal determination might have helped set me above the others of my year but, if it did, Tom never said so, and nor did he give me first crack when the four of us were thought ready for a racecourse outing. Naturally, there was an element of competition between us. It never became nasty but it was often evident for, after all, what we were contesting might easily have been one opening into the jockeys' world, one career.

And that was how it turned out, though at first it did not look as if I would be the recipient.

After four months at Green Lodge I had begun riding work on a serious basis. After a year, I was a regular, scarcely missing out on our two main work days, Wednesday and Saturday. But as the 1973 flat season began, I had still not been promised a race-ride and nor had I been allowed to help schooling the jumpers. I chafed resentfully.

Already, I think, my heart was in the winter game. When the National Hunt season came, Stan Mellor and David Mould were regular morning visitors, schooling the horses they would eventually ride in public. My face lit up every time they came and I would happily hang around on the schooling grounds in freezing cold weather, just mesmerised by the sight of my heroes in person. We schooled once each week and I could barely contain my impatience to try it myself.

I had been with Tom for three years before he unleashed me on the schooling grounds and, by then, I had ridden in a flat race for the first and only time as an apprentice.

We had a three-year-old filly called Fine Leg, who was not very speedy but, being well-balanced and well-behaved, was an ideal apprentices' ride. Paul Booth was given the first ride on her, then came Peter Green. I had to content myself with being third in line and, having been given a few days' notice of the big day, I also had to do some serious wasting. I had weighed seven stone ten pounds when I went to Newmarket as a fifteen-year-old but I was now approaching eighteen and my weight had gone up to eight stone seven. Fine Leg was to run with eight stone three pounds and, to meet the weight, I did not eat a thing for three days. I also went running in garb I would only recommend to someone seeking drastic weight loss. I wore a Sketchley plastic bag next to my skin, then put on a T-shirt, sweatshirt, jumper and waterproof jacket. Although it was springtime and the weather was mild, I also donned a pair of gloves and a woolly hat, as I had been told that heat can easily escape through your head and fingers. You do not need to run very far to lose a pound or two in this sort of uniform but, as I discovered, you are also likely to attract some pitying stares.

I made the weight and kept the ride. The race was at Yarmouth, one of the more local tracks from Newmarket, and I went in the horsebox with our travelling head lad, Ian Wardle. I kept looking at the racing papers and checking the Yarmouth card, just to make sure it was my name against Fine Leg, just below that of Lester Piggott.

It would be wrong to claim I was not nervous. As I sat in the changing room, glancing round at all the famous faces, my knees had turned to a very watery jelly. Equally, it might have been worse. If the race had been run, as all flat races are nowadays, from a stalls start, I would have been terrified, because my efforts at putting horses through the stalls at home had not been very impressive. Luck had it (or more likely, Tom Jones had organised it) that my debut was to be made from a barrier start, and that eased the nerves appreciably.

I had no chance of winning. Even I was realistic enough to accept that. I beat two home and felt smugly self-satisfied to have done so well. But my abiding memory from the race was that it was over almost before I was aware it had begun. There was a sensation of speed I had never known, even on the gallops back home, and it seemed that within two blinks of an eye, three beats of a heart, we were pulling up again.

Back at the yard, there was a swagger in my step for a day or two. After one ride, I imagined I was a jockey. But the democracy of the environment soon disabused me of that notion. I was simply given some extra mucking-out to do. Stable life was like that. It is all about building a character. Every time a lad gets above himself, he is knocked back down again. You resent it at the time but it has to be that way and, after five years of it, I reckon it is as good an education for life as there is available.

Chapter Three

Dear Mum, Dad and Diane,
Received your letter today. Miss you very much. Looking forward to seeing you next Sunday.

I would appreciate it very much if you could send me a £1 every week as I usually go to the pictures and pub once a week, being as all the lads are little they let us in to all the Xs.

Love Stephen

3 September 1970

Dear Mum, Dad and Diane,
Hope you are managing well with the strike. Well, anyway, I'm sending you a £1. Hope it comes in handy.

Hope you was watching BBC1 on Friday afternoon, if so you would have seen me leading up Vulgan's Arms at Ascot...

I will send you some more money as soon as I can and the sooner this strike ends the better. If it keeps on I suppose the schools will shut down through lack of coke for the central heating. That should suit our Diane.

Love Steve

21 January 1972

Dear Mum, Dad and Diane,
I have finished with Lesley. I told her I thought we'd been going with each other for too long, so I'm on the loose again.

... I'm decorating the interior of a house all this week for this young lady I know in the next village...

Lots of love Steve

28 January 1974

[Changing moods, changing times, reflected in letters home.]

It had taken me a couple of months to find my feet in New-market. No more. In that time, to this completely unworldly fifteen-year-old, the place had seemed as homely and welcoming as an alien planet. Then came the dawning realisation that I was no longer a boy, but a young man who had stumbled upon an Aladdin's Cave.

By day I was discovering, albeit slowly, the exhilarations of the job which was never to lose its mesmeric appeal. By night, I was unleashed upon a whole new world, delightfully unfamiliar, in which girls and alcohol were readily on tap in about equal volume.

You can never tell what you will make of a new situation until it actually confronts you. By background and breeding, I was a pretty unlikely addition to the ranks of the racing fraternity, yet their lifestyle fitted me like a glove. It was active and outdoors, which I think for me were two prerequisites. And it was sociable in an earthy, unpretentious, make-of-it-what-you-can way which, from that day to this, has always been my style. No one has ever accused me of being an angel but equally, I hope, no one has detected any malice in me. I have boundless energy and a will to enjoy life. Newmarket contained any number of kindred spirits.

Ma Coogan's digs had some severe shortcomings, as I have already explained, but she never had any shortage of takers. Newmarket is an overpopulated town and there is a constant influx of lads and lasses seeking somewhere to live. Almost without exception, they have no money in their pocket so they take what is available. Landladies like Ma Coogan had a good thing going in those days and, to the best of my knowledge, still do.

The house in Nat Flatman Street might have seemed gross to me, when I arrived straight from the protective arm of the family home, but it was actually typical of dozens in the town. Old Ma had four children herself but these were heavily outnumbered by nine or ten stable-lads and apprentices. At £8 per week per head, this represented very handy money in the early 1970s.

Once I got used to the food and the confinements of six to a room, it was also far from the worst place in which I laid my head during those early years. What it most had in its favour was a good position. I am not talking estate agent language here. I don't mean it boasted tranquil seclusion and an unrivalled aspect of rolling fields. It certainly did not. But it met the most pressing desires of its inmates by having a chip shop directly opposite and a pub twenty yards to one side. The slight handicap was that the building twenty yards the other side was the police station but this was something we learned, cautiously, to live with.

It was in this local pub that I began to drink whisky for the first time. I still drink it now, and, although I tell people it is far better for my weight than drinking beer, it is really because I enjoy it a lot more.

I was, of course, still only fifteen but one of my earliest and most wondrous discoveries was that, once working in Newmarket, you could get a drink in the town pubs no matter what your age. By the nature of the racing game, everyone working in the yards is small and I think pub landlords gave up years ago trying to differentiate between those who might be tiny and fifteen and those who were the same height but ten years older. They just served the drinks and took the money. The problems arose when it came to going racing, for those in charge of the racecourse bars were not so cavalier. I have known lads in their mid-twenties refused a drink on a racecourse because they did not look eighteen.

Afternoons were habitually spent in the bookies. Jockeys are forbidden to bet by the rules of racing but stable-lads can back every horse in their yard if they choose to, and many do. Every bookmaker's shop in Newmarket was packed once racing began and there was not much in the way of passing trade. This was the lads' meeting point, where gossip would be swapped along with tips for the afternoon's sport. The trouble was that there were always far too many tips flying around, most of them inevitably duff. But with our two-bob yankees and our little each-ways, the occasional touch did come off and there was always smug celebrating when one of Tom Jones's horses went in.

25

This intermingling between the yards continued after dark and it was then that it could become less than friendly. There was always plenty of scrapping but it came less from a need or wish to fight than from basic tribal instincts, an effort to establish a pecking order between the tribes, or yards, in the town. It seldom seemed serious, at least to us, because we were all in the same job together. But when the yanks hit town, that was a different matter.

We were paid every Thursday and the idea would be to put a few bob away for the rest of the week before blowing most of the wages on three decent nights out. From our local pubs, we would descend quickly upon the Stable Lads' Institute, where the food and drink were dirt cheap. The night would end up in one of the town's discos – if it was Thursday, it might be the Memorial Hall, Friday All Saints' Hall. On Saturday, almost without fail, the majority of us would turn up at the Doric Hotel, a big, Georgian gin palace in the High Street. The Doric was a very attractive building, had we bothered to notice. It had a big, marble dance floor, with a balustrade circling it and a glass-domed ceiling. On Saturday nights, though, the marble was sprinkled with sawdust. The proprietors knew it would not be a genteel occasion.

Newmarket is surrounded by air bases and, every Saturday night, the American airmen from Mildenhall, Lakenham and Alconbury came into town and headed for the Doric. It was an accepted thing, almost an honoured tradition, that the evening could not end without a fight between the airmen and the stable-lads.

Being young, small and, perhaps, a touch canny, I would usually melt into the dimly lit background once hostilities began, arming myself with a bottle just in case any yank came close enough to try something on. But, week after week, I went back and wondered at this Wild West scene, bodies strewn among broken glass until, inevitably, the police moved wearily in to call a halt, like a referee blowing the final whistle at a football match. There were always any number of minor cuts and bruises at the end of the contest but I remember, one night, seeing an American being hurled from the balcony. It was a fair drop down to the marble floor and a hard landing, too. The airman broke his leg and suffered quite severe head injuries. It never seemed quite such fun after that.

The Doric has gone now, knocked down years back, but the landmarks of my first lodgings are all still standing – the police station, where officers doubtless berated the irresponsibility of the local youth, the pub and the chip shop. And Ma Coogan's house on the corner of Nat Flatman Street is still there, too. Whenever I pass, I wonder if she is still taking in lodgers and dropping fag-ash in the lunchtime stews.

I stayed there for three months and left for no other reason than wanting to better myself. I was certain I could find something less cramped and more comfortable, somewhere I could feel more at home. Initially, at least, I could not have been more wrong.

There was a lad called Arthur working for Tom Jones and he told me there was a vacancy at his digs. Arthur said he had been there more than four years and thought of it as home. There were only two lads to a room, he said, and I could share with him. He spoke highly of the place and, not bothering to check it out any further, I took him at face value, packed up and left Ma Coogan and carried my suitcase around to an imposing house in Rous Road.

Another tight-lipped woman, typical of the breed, I was beginning to think, answered my knock and showed me up to the room I was to share with Arthur. If the woman had waited, I am sure my astonishment would have betrayed me but, with little interest in the affair, she was off downstairs again to read the *Daily Mirror*. I stared around at my new domain and saw that there were, indeed, only two beds in the room. The bad news was that they were both fragile camp beds and that they comprised the entire furnishings of the room. There was nothing else at all, not a table, a chair or even a mirror or picture to brighten up the drab, greying walls. And here was another thing. Closer inspection revealed that the walls and ceiling were damp and mildewed. A cursory inspection of the bedclothes confirmed my worst fears.

Arthur was not present when I checked into the establishment and, as I stood there still clutching my old suitcase in bemusement, I got to marvelling at his fortitude in staying in this room for four years, when the only indication it might be his home was that his clothes were piled up on the floor between the beds. As for me, I could not envisage spending four nights there, much less four years, and as I drowned my sorrows in the pub that evening, my conviction grew that I would be looking for fresh digs again the following day.

I made sure I anaesthetised myself with whisky that night, and when I crept apprehensively back into my uninviting room, I slept fully clothed on top of the rickety camp bed. Hangover or not, I was up early next morning, picking up the case I had not even bothered to unpack and escaping from Rous Road before the landlady had even stirred from her bed. I hoped for her sake it was not as damp as mine, I thought fleetingly as I gratefully took my leave.

Sunday morning was spent in vain, foot-slogging pursuit of a replacement room. Some lodgings were full, others might not have liked the look of me, preferring to have their apprentices sent on by trainers. Whatever the reason, I failed at every port of call and, as late afternoon brought winter darkness to the town, I fell back on my last resort.

The tack room at Green Lodge was not exactly the Dorchester but it was familiar ground and it had certain definite plus points. I knew it was vacant and I knew it would be warm. I crept back into the yard, collected some of the spare horse rugs and settled down under them next to the stove which burned away there all winter.

The other lads, arriving early next morning, found me still asleep and, curiously, asked me what I had been doing. 'Playing cards with the rats' was the most mysterious quip I could come up with. In fact I had slept surprisingly well and, although the cold tap in the yard did not provide the most luxurious washing facilities, I still felt I was better off than back in Rous Road. Unbeknown to Tom Jones, who would decidedly not have approved, I slept in the tack room every night for a week, allowing myself one break from the tap by taking a shower at the Lads' Institute. When the weekend came around again, I moved on.

In the course of three or four years I probably went through ten sets of digs. I never stayed long anywhere and, although some of my moves were voluntary, others were enforced. One landlady, a Mrs Stanford, kicked me out because she said I splashed too much water around whenever I took a bath. If I left that house with a self-righteous sense of grievance, I knew the next landlady who told me to leave had a better case. She accused me of seducing her teenage daughter. And she was right. Next stop was with a married couple recently moved into the area from Birmingham. This time, I was the innocent party, brazenly seduced by the brassy woman of the house. I left before the husband's suspicion turned to agitation.

I guess my parents, accustomed to spending a lifetime in a village, were bewildered by the constant changes of address. There were times when they sounded genuinely worried about me when they wrote but, the pangs of homesickness having disappeared from my own letters pretty early on, I would always reassure them that all was well. Before long, they had a telephone installed back at Pinxton and it became the custom for me to ring them every Sunday evening. It is now twenty-three years since I left home but that custom remains and I still faithfully make the Sunday phone call to fill them in with all my news and check on their own health.

They came over to Newmarket every couple of months during my years as an apprentice. We always arranged it for my free Sunday and we developed a routine we all enjoyed. For lunch, we went to the Palace Café. It was an unprepossessing place in the backstreets of town but I had discovered that they served up a delicious, three-course Sunday lunch for the princely sum of five shillings. There was always a good soup to start, then roast beef, with apple pie and custard for pudding. Dad loved it. We would walk off the excess on the heath before they went back, their heads filled with my carefully selective stories of the apprentices' lifestyle.

I did not, for instance, introduce them to my first real girl-friend. Nor did I tell them of the first occasion I had got to know her intimately. Her name was Lesley and I had taken her to a pub on a Thursday night, making sure she had enough to drink to lose any inhibitions. She did not seem to need much further encouragement but, as it was strictly forbidden to take girls back to my lodgings (a rule even I struggled to evade more than occasionally), sex was necessarily an outdoor pursuit.

At the end of Lesley's back garden there were two garages, with a narrow alleyway between them. It was dark there, which suited our purposes well, and if it was also cold with one of the winter's early frosts threatening, we simply considered that an inducement to getting warm. I laid my Levi jacket on the concrete and laid Lesley down on top of it. All was going well until we were unexpectedly disturbed. There was a man heading unsteadily our way between the garages. He was a big fellow and he had obviously been in the pub a good few hours. He was also Lesley's father.

We lay where we were, frozen by terror rather than temperature. This big, gruff old boy peered at us, swaying drunkenly at a sight he had not bargained for on his usual short-cut home at chucking-out time. Then, with breathless relief, I saw that there was no recognition in his eyes. With a sudden snort of laughter, he staggered on, bouncing off one of the garages as he slurred over his shoulder, 'Go on, my son. Give her one for me.'

Lesley and I did not take such a chance on that particular shady spot again but I went on seeing her for a while. I was not, however, of a mind to make a steady relationship at that time. I was by now aware that plenty of young girls worked in racing stables and, for reasons that I never quite managed to explain, most of them regarded sex as a desirable commodity in almost any environment, rather than something to be saved for a special occasion. These were pre-Aids days and there was nothing prudish or prudent about the passion and frequency of Newmarket-based relationships.

The best days of all were those spent at the races. Every apprentice, every lad and lass, accompanies the horses they 'do' when they run. This heightens the competition for the best and most prolific horses, as there is not much to be said for doing a broken down old thing who might manage a couple of runs in selling plates at Yarmouth when you might be responsible for one of the jump season's top novices, bound for Sandown, Ascot, Cheltenham and Liverpool.

I got a trip to Liverpool in my first year with Tom Jones. The road network, of course, was nothing like it is today and any trip of that distance demanded an overnight stay. On these occasions, we lads were given a pound for expenses, which was quite enough to have a decent night out and come home with five bob in your pocket. But my memory of that first time at Liverpool is of the lads' hostel. It was a cavernous dormitory with Army-type camp beds covered by damp sheets. There was dirt on the floor and in the washbasins and it was always bitterly cold. How we did not all catch pneumonia, if not some more sinister disease, is beyond me. How I ever got to sleep at night, with a dozen or more strangers snoring, was mystery enough. Our travelling head lad, Ian Wardle, went to the same Derbyshire school as I had done, albeit twelve years earlier, and this broke the ice between us for a friendship which has survived all manner of ups and downs in our two lives. These days, he is my agent, booking my rides. Back in the early 1970s, he knew enough of the right sort of people to make an overnight stop at some far-flung racecourse a positive pleasure.

I hit the jackpot one week when Tom Jones declared one of my horses to run at Teesside. This would have entailed an overnight stop in any case but it was a two-day meeting and the guv'nor had runners both days. So Ian and I set off in the box, along with the two horses and a lass called Monica, for a two-night stay in the north-east. It was an area of the country I had never visited but Ian, needless to say, had planned ahead. When he dropped me at the hostel he told me to be ready at 6.30 p.m. as we were going to the greyhound track. He also told me to bring all the money I had with me. I took ten shillings, leaving enough to feed myself for the rest of the stay. I was resigned to losing the ten bob, knowing nothing about dog racing, but when Ian picked me up, he had with him two guys who ran the track. Smoothly, they took my racecard, marked off a few dogs and returned it with a knowing wink. The upshot was that I backed eight consecutive winners and won £10.

Not every racing trip was as perfect as this one (my horse won and I scored with Monica in the box on the journey home!), but plenty more were memorable and almost all were educational, in their way. And, while I continued to learn about racing, its people and its customs, I also learned rapidly about life.

One of the great truths, I discovered, was that Newmarket was full of frustrated women and that not all of them were good news. I am thinking particularly of the night when I, and some of the other lads, were invited to a party given by a fellow called Ron, his wife and her sister.

Ron was a boxer, and built for it, so there was no way I was looking to try anything on with his wife. I had half a notion that the sister fancied me, in fact, but as the night went on and the drinks went down, the time came when I ceased to care. I set off upstairs to the loo without a thought in my head apart from the obvious, but no sooner was I inside the door than I found another body squeezing in behind mine. To my great surprise it was Ron's wife, and she was plainly not there to have an argument about who could use the loo first.

She soon had me pressed up against the wall, my trousers round my ankles. I was too flattered to protest and too drunk to think of the danger. Until, that is, there was a resounding bang on the door and Ron's unmistakable voice demanded to know what Mrs Ron was up to. Chillingly, he added, 'And where's that bloody little Eccles?' I didn't wait for any further social pleasantries. When the bones in your body are suddenly at risk of being crushed to a pulp, it is amazing how fast one can sober up, not to mention hitch up discarded trousers and pants. Looking up desperately, I identified my means of escape as the small window. It was barely big enough for anyone to get through but, propelled by dread, I went through it head first, almost without touching the sides.

We were on the first floor but there was a drainpipe outside the loo. I clutched it gratefully as I emerged from my bolt-hole, slid a few feet and then dropped the rest of the way, landing awkwardly but safely on hands and knees. As I made off up the garden, I heard the loo door burst open, a clamour of raised voices and what sounded suspiciously like a blow struck in anger. Then Ron's head came through the escape-hatch window and he bellowed after me, 'I'll get you, you little bastard.' I hardly went out for the next month!

It was to be some while before I dropped roots to any degree but the closest I came was when I spent a year lodging with Tom Jones's regular apprentice jockey, Jock Ferguson, who, by this time, was living with Ian Wardle's first wife, Lynn. That tangled web was to become still more complicated but it was still a happy place for me and it was also the scene of my twenty-first birthday party, an all-day and all-night affair notable for a £5 bet struck between Tommy Keddy and myself over how many girls we could each lay during the festivities. He scored four and lost.

That, curiously, was the night I met Di Walton, the girl who was to become my wife. We first rented a flat together for a couple of years and then, the nuptials arranged, I bought my first house in the village of Moulton, just outside Newmarket.

I was having my wings clipped, losing the independence I had come to relish. I think I knew, even on my wedding day, that it was an ill-fated venture. I virtually said as much to John Francome, sitting beside me in church as my best man. His reply was that he had forked out £25 to hire a morning suit and he was damned if he was going to waste the money by letting me call it off now.

The way things worked out, I dearly wish I had got out my wallet there and then, given him his money back and scarpered. The marriage lasted less than a year. There will be plenty who are not remotely surprised.

Chapter Four

Dear Mrs Smith Eccles,

Just a line to reassure you about Stephen. He's doing a first-class job here and we all think a lot of him. He's quite right in saying that this job takes time but I really think he is making very good progress. I have applied for an apprentice's licence for him to ride this season and hope to get him started with a ride or two as soon as possible. He will have a certain amount of competition from other apprentices but I think he'll stand up to that all right. He's a pretty determined character!

Very best wishes,
Yours sincerely,
Tom Jones

March 1972

Dear Mum, Dad and Diane,

I went in to see the governor today about learning to shcool [sic] horses over the jumps and these are the exact words he replied. 'That's a splendid idea, that's exactly what I want you to do, I'll have to get you started straight away. Just pop your skull cap in my car boot.'

So, I should be riding a bit of schooling when I get back off my holidays.

Lots of love Steve

August 1972

Dear Mum, Dad and Diane,

... About you sending another letter to Jones. I think it's a very good idea but be very careful what you put. Come to think about it you can put what you like, he doesn't seem very interested in giving me rides so how the hell can he expect me to be interested...

Lots of love Steve

February 1974

I spent five years as an apprentice with Tom Jones and another four years riding most of his jumpers. I later lived with his daughter for eight years and spent each Christmas Day with him. Yet through it all he has remained the one trainer I will never address by his Christian name. I have never called him Tom to his face and I am sure I never will. The master–apprentice relationship is an enduring one and, to me, Tom Jones will always be 'guv'nor' or 'sir'. He will also be the man who made me. I owe him my career.

There were plenty of times when I cursed him. He could seem a tyrant and he often seemed unreasonably reluctant to allow me my head. Only in retrospect can these things be appreciated. Tom Jones taught me respect, which is essential in this job, and by bringing me on at the pace he dictated, rather than the pace I would have preferred, he was teaching me patience. If he had let me do everything I wanted, when I wanted it, I am prepared to believe I would have blown my chances. I think my enthusiasm and total commitment had its impression on the guv'nor and, from what I have heard since, I believe he had also identified a spark of ability in my riding at a fairly early stage. He was not a man to say as much, though, and nor would it influence his methods. He had been in the game long enough to assess when a lad was ready, mentally as well as technically, to take each step up the ladder. In my case, hard though I thought him at the time, I think he got it absolutely right.

I wonder if the boss ever tired of me hassling him. I lost count of the number of times I went to see him to ask if I could begin to ride the jumpers at schooling. It was the same, later, when I felt I was good enough and old enough to race-ride over hurdles. On every occasion, he kept me waiting until he, the guv'nor, was ready. From the time I arrived in Newmarket, my head had told me that the jumping game was for me, primarily because I knew I would never be light enough to sustain a career on the flat. But after a couple of years at Green Lodge, my heart told me the same thing. The flat had certain things going for it, such as summertime and speed, but I had been captivated by the sight and sound of horses jumping, and it was a fascination that was to stay with me.

My badgering of the guv'nor probably had no effect but eventually, of course, he made up his own mind that I could be introduced to the schooling grounds as a participant rather than an avid spectator. I was allowed to ride the stable hack, leading some three-year-olds over the first obstacles they had ever jumped. It was nothing more daunting than a set of poles but it was the first important step. Next, again on the hack, I led the novices over miniature hurdles up on the Links. Only after that did I graduate to full-size hurdles, but always on the lead horse and for very good reason. He might never have been a star and he was certainly not built for speed any more, but he was vastly experienced. So, while he was teaching the young horses the rudiments of jumping, he was also teaching his young rider. Park Ranger was his name and I remember him fondly.

David Mould was the stable-jockey by this time and I could not have asked for a more considerate man to help me long. It was David, having watched me schooling one day, who took me aside and told me the great secret of riding over obstacles. You must always be looking for a stride, he said. I didn't have the first idea what he meant, and I think my expression told him so. But he was a kind man and he took the time to explain. Twenty yards from the hurdle or fence, he said, your horse has maybe three more strides before he has to take off. You must learn to be ahead of him, to gauge that distance and to know where you want to be taking off. Once you are in tune with the horse's stride you know whether to sit still, if he is on target, take a pull if he is getting in close, or give him a kick in the belly if you need him to take off from half-a-length further back. When the penny dropped, the whole business of jumping suddenly seemed more straightforward. And yet, when I look around today, I see plenty of full-time professional jockeys for whom the penny plainly never has dropped at all!

No sooner had I begun schooling on a regular basis than I was agitating for race rides. That, however, was to be a year away and, in the meantime, the unglamorous side of stable life continued as before. I was still shifting from one digs to another, still making a small wage go a remarkably long way on the Newmarket social circuit and, not being the retiring sort, still having my share of bust-ups within working hours.

One of the worst involved Michael Stoute. These days, Michael is among the two or three most eminent trainers in the land. He still bases himself in Newmarket and we get along fine. Back in the early 1970s, however, he had not long arrived in England from his native Barbados when he came to our yard as assistant trainer and, in two years, he made the lads' life hell.

As a general rule, assistant trainers can be unpopular with the lads because, although they wield authority, they seldom command respect. They are the hired help rather than the master, and the difference is marked. Michael caused particular resentment by the manner in which he treated us, and, although my lowly position gave me no right of reply whatever, I never have been the type to act like a servile mute if I feel I am being wronged. I reacted, verbally, more than once, and Michael eventually exploded, pinning me up against a stable wall. He did not hit me, which was just as well as he is a big and powerful man, but for as long as he remained at Green Lodge our relationship was simmering with mutual dislike. Michael has certainly changed since then; probably, I have too.

Among the other assistants who passed through the place during my years were Alec Stewart, another highly regarded trainer these days, and John Ciekanowski, Polish-born, French-speaking and a man who later trod diverse paths in racing, including a couple of unsuccessful training stints. I like John a lot, and still see him about the place, but as assistant he was known for doing everything by the book, to a pedantic degree.

Saturday was one of our gallops mornings but it was seldom a day on which Tom Jones rose feeling at his best. I think Friday night on the town may have had a little to do with the fact that he was quite often late on parade, but work never started until he arrived and John Ciekanowski would insist that we all stayed on our mounts, taking a turn. This process would sometimes extend to fifteen or twenty minutes, in which there would be some general grumbling about the likelihood of Ciekanowski taking a turn in his grave.

One day, after a typical bout of this charade, we were finally ready to go. I was scheduled to set off after John, who was riding a decent but headstrong gelding called French Society. The accepted rule when cantering jumpers, as we were that day, is to stay about thirty yards behind the horse in front. Instead, I took my mount right up behind French Society until, as we turned the bend at the foot of the hill, I clicked my tongue encouragingly, with the result I had hoped for. French Society took off, John quite unable to restrain him, and as they passed Tom Jones, standing by his car three furlongs up the hill, John was still shouting and screaming abuse in my general direction. I had by this time retreated to the regulation thirty yards but what I could not do was control my mirth. By the time I came level with the guv'nor, there were tears of laughter streaming down my face. Unhappily, one glance was enough to confirm my fears that Tom Jones was not sharing the joke.

He came down hard on me for that prank but he was not a man to bear grudges or be vindictive. Nor did he discourage my increasingly frequent forays into his office. My campaign for a ride over hurdles was now in full swing and, every Sunday morning, when I knew the boss did the runners for the coming week, I would go in and plead my case. He always listened but never committed himself until, as Christmas approached in the 1973–74 season, I thought the moment had come. Boxing Day is the busiest of the year for many jumping trainers and we were not alone in planning runners far and wide. This puts an annual strain on riding resources and, as he perused his provisional list, the guv'nor said he thought he could find me a ride somewhere. I left his office on cloud nine.

Christmas Eve dawned and nothing more had been said. In some trepidation, I asked him where I might be riding. He replied that he had been unable to find anything suitable. I gawped at him foolishly and could think of nothing to say. I had already allowed myself to get so excited at the prospect that this sudden, fickle disenchantment left me feeling physically sick.

It had been planned that Mum and Dad would drop by that afternoon and give me my Christmas presents. When they arrived, wreathed in festive smiles and carrying a bag stuffed with parcels,

I was brusque, ungracious and straight to the point. 'Don't bother unpacking them,' I said, 'we're going home.'

Saying nothing to Tom Jones, or to anyone else for that matter, I simply got in the family car and went back to Derbyshire. Mum and Dad were part puzzled, part concerned at what I was doing, but my disillusionment was such that I no longer cared. I honestly believed I would never be going back to Newmarket and that my racing dreams were now consigned, unfulfilled, to history.

It was a brooding, bad tempered sort of Christmas, not helped by the sight of the Boxing Day racecards in the papers, and the resentful feeling that so many other lads were getting their chance ahead of me. After about four days, I began to weaken. Had I done the right thing? What would I do now to avoid going down the pit? And, finally, could I go back and find my job still waiting for me? Encouraged by Mum and Dad, who were anxious I should not throw away three-and-a-half years' hard slog, I set off to find out.

My tail was trailing between my legs when I reported to Tom Jones and I remained sheepishly contrite throughout the ensuing interview. He tore me off a strip, and was well entitled to do so. It had been the performance of a spoiled and arrogant lad, which I hoped I was not. It had also been the performance of a deeply frustrated one, and I was certainly that. In one sense, however, I think my over-reaction had a desirable effect. It drew attention to me and, although I might at the moment of my return have been embarrassed by that, it was a fact that from then on I did more and more schooling and that, later that year, I had my first ride.

Going home for Christmas might not have been the most mature or sensible thing to do but it was a kind of cry for help. The help I wanted duly arrived, though from an unexpected source.

Jimmy Scallan was a Newmarket-based jockey who rode out regularly for Tom Jones and rode some of the hurdlers in their races. His afternoons were spent at a less exalted racing establishment out in the Fens, where a permit holder named Bob Finch trained a handful of moderate animals. One of them was called Turalini and, when he was entered for a novice hurdle at Huntingdon, Jimmy was routinely put down for the ride.

Complications arose when Tom Jones decided to run a three-year-old called Tempered Steel in the same race. I did Tempered Steel and he was not a bad novice. Jimmy had already won on him a couple of times and was naturally keen to keep the ride. His solution was to recommend to Bob Finch that I should take over for the day on Turalini. Finch agreed, so too did my guv'nor, but prior to race-day, I was to go and sit on Turalini, just to get the feel of him. Jimmy Scallan drove me out there for the exercise, which involved riding this hairy, unimpressive little horse, barely bigger than a Shetland pony, round what looked very like a cabbage patch. Newmarket it was not, but why should I have cared? My big moment had come and I was not about to quibble about the quality of the horse or the standard of facilities.

Huntingdon is the most local jumping course to Newmarket and it has been a lucky track for me over the years. My first stroke of luck, when I walked into the weighing-room, was to bump straight into John Buckingham. 'Buck', forever famous for piloting Foinavon through the carnage at the twenty-third fence to win the 1967 Grand National, had retired from riding to become a jockeys' valet. Each of the valets operates independently and can lay a permanent claim on a jockey by grabbing him on his first day. 'Who are you,' asked John, studying his racecard for clues. 'My name's Steve Eccles,' I replied with a touch of pride. 'Right, you'd better come with me,' he said. And that was that. 'Buck' has been my valet from that day to this and, quite apart from ministering to all my equipment needs and generally fussing over me, he is a true and valued friend.

As he looked me up and down on that first day, I should not imagine it entered Buck's head that we might still be together almost twenty years later. I was just another aspiring rider to kit out, and it was well known that the great majority fell quickly by the wayside. I didn't even have my own breeches and boots. 'Buck' supplied those, breeches which made me look like a First World War airman and boots which were so big they had to be held on with elastic bands. But even before I had ridden in my first National Hunt race, I had no doubt that I would become a fixture.

There is a traditional pecking order in the weighing-room, the senior, most experienced jockey getting the privileged number-one peg and the newest of the new boys getting the draughty seat next to the door. 'Buck' pointed me to the right peg and, as

I sat down, my eyes took in the scene until they rested on the number-one seat, occupied with his usual massive bonhomie by Terry Biddlecombe. I clearly remember saying to myself, 'I'm going to sit in that seat one day.' It was breathtaking over-confidence from one who had yet to ride a race, let alone a winner, and nowadays, sitting as I do in that number one position, I occasionally look across to the seat by the door and wonder if the fresh-faced new boy there is having the same outrageous thought.

I had been strongly advised to walk the course before racing and I was glad to do so, not just to acquaint myself with the lay-out but because my senses were so alert that I wanted to take everything in. On that special day, nothing was mundane, everything was picked out in sudden dramatic detail, from the smell of the grass to the colour of the hurdles. The sight of the grandstand beginning to fill up excited me and I sauntered back into the weighing-room feeling, I suppose, like an actor on first night. There were no nerves as such, for I have never suffered that way. Just an overwhelming sense of expectancy, the certainty that something memorable was about to take place.

I was not wrong in that, although it did not take place in the way the best of dreams would have had it. I was down at the start almost before I knew it, the parade-ring ceremony having passed in a blur, instructions from the trainer inevitably forgotten as soon as spoken. I recall some of the old lags of the game approaching me as we circled, perusing this new kid on the block and gruffly asking where I intended to be in the race. As I mumbled something noncommittal, they would invariably add, 'Just stay out of my bloody way.' It was new to me, and slightly intimidating, but it was no more than ritual.

Although my secret subconscious was probably harbouring absurd notions of a winning debut, I had no realistic chance in the race and I knew it. Turalini had run once before, down the field, and even Bob Finch himself had not pretended that he was likely to do any better this time. My priority was to get round safely. As it turned out, I almost got no further than the first hurdle.

I jumped off in a respectful position, not exactly jousting for the lead but not last either, and concentrated on putting my horse right for the all-important first. Remember David Mould's lesson, I was telling myself, look for the stride and act on it. No matter how many sessions one may have had on the schooling grounds, however, it is no preparation for the hurly-burly of a novice hurdle, in which the anxiety of every jockey to gain daylight for his mount is compounded by the antics of the inexperienced horses.

As we approached the hurdle, a horse in front of me darted across our path. Turalini jinked, clambering over the hurdle at an awkward angle and twisting in mid-air. I was flung sideways out of the saddle, and had reached that point of no return, when a hand reached out from alongside me and shoved me back on board.

Gathering my composure and my reins, re-uniting my feet with the irons and thanking my lucky stars, I threw one quick, grateful glance at my helper. I didn't know him, but I would know him again, sooner than I expected.

Any competitive interest in the race had departed for me with that first-flight mishap but, thankful to be continuing, I schooled Turalini round the rest of the course and turned into the home straight for the last time with just the one hurdle left to clear. He was hanging into the rails, which did not disturb me, and there was another horse just in front, running up the middle inner of the track. I recognised the colours, and the face, of my fairy godfather but discovered that he was not quite the philanthropist he had seemed.

My horse was going marginally less slowly than his by this time and carrying me into the hurdle on the inside of him. Without warning, my erstwhile friend came violently across and rammed me into the wing of the obstacle. We staggered across it somehow, the air full of cries from yours truly. The answer to my agonised query as to what the hell he was doing was quite simple. 'Just practising, son,' he said. 'Don't try and come up my inner again.'

In those days, a jockey could get away with such acts of villainy. There were no SIS cameras and the ordinary stewards' patrol camera was hopelessly inadequate. The law of the jungle prevailed, the weak going to the wall, for if you tried to pass on the inside, and were not quick enough or good enough, you would sure as hell end up in the rails. This, however, was one of the more pointless examples I ever did see, one tailed-off horse savaging another for the sake of it. Practising indeed!

Tempered Steel had won the race, but I returned to weigh in happy to be back in one piece and to have gained a valuable motto. Trust nobody in a race, even a man bearing gifts. I have often looked back to that race, though, and wondered what might have happened to me if my Jekyll and Hyde colleague, who shall remain unnamed, had not intervened at the first hurdle. The sheer ignominy of it might have been too much for me. It could even have put me off the game for life. Somehow, I doubt it.

Chapter Five

'Much of the credit for Swift Shadow's success must go to Steve Smith Eccles, who quickened and slowed the pace with the dexterity of a Lester Piggott, and gave a riding performance that was a joy to watch.'

'... Tingle Creek and Smith Eccles were given a tremendous reception on their return to the winners' enclosure. It was almost reminiscent of the days of the mighty Arkle...'

Sporting Life, 5 December 1977

First impressions are important with any would-be employer and, as a young jockey beginning to chase spare rides, I started out with quite a disadvantage. I had no telephone. Day after day, I would pore endlessly over the advance declarations in the *Sporting Life* and identify possible spares. It was when it came to contacting the relevant trainers that I found things difficult. The public call-box was not a great medium for a sales pitch.

Many were the times that I filled my jeans pockets with coins and set off to the nearest unvandalised kiosk, *Sporting Life* and list of telephone numbers tucked under my arm. Impatient though I was to make my mark, I never stepped out of my depth. Recognising the futility of phoning the likes of Fred Winter or Fulke Walwyn, I focused my attentions on obscure trainers, usually based in remote rural parts and invariably without a retained jockey of their own.

I had a standard speech rehearsed to try and emphasise my credentials and there was a certain amount of licence in the self-flattery department. But it was disconcerting enough to have the constant suspicion that the trainer at the other end was only half listening to my oratory, let alone to be interrupted by the pips, requiring an undignified scramble to insert further coins.

It surprises me, with hindsight, that I came away with a ride as often as I did, although it would be a fabrication to suggest I was ever overbooked. Any fanciful notion that my debut sixth, on Turalini at Huntingdon, might bring a flow of rides from admiring trainers, was instantly dispelled. There were times when I had serious doubts about from where, or even if, the next ride would come.

The second ride was not a problem. It came thirteen days after the first and the booking was for a three-mile hurdle at, of all places, Cheltenham. It was not a very promising conveyance, a seven-year-old called Moss Flower with no obvious form, trained by a Welsh hill farmer. So far as I was concerned, this was secondary to the fact that I was to ride at the headquarters of the sport, and in a race which was to be televised live. I phoned home the previous evening, just to make sure all the family would be watching, but I need not have bothered. It would have taken a lot to make them miss it.

I was learning to drive by this time but I still had no car of my own, so I was grateful when the guv'nor, who had runners at the meeting, offered me a lift. I still remember his car breasting the top of Cleeve Hill, opening up that spectacular vista across the town to the Malverns, the racecourse dominating the foreground. My stomach churned at the sight.

It was the day before the Mackeson Gold Cup, so there was a decent crowd in, and the air of expectancy around the place was a thrill and an education. I had no more chance of winning than I had at Huntingdon, probably considerably less, but at least I made sure I was mentioned on TV by making the running for the first mile-and-a-half. I just hope that some of the viewers were unaware that I was in front on sufferance, the horse having run away with me as soon as the tapes went up.

Exactly four months were to pass before my next ride. Frustration is not the word. Throughout my life, I have wanted things to happen yesterday; tomorrow has always been too long to wait.

I imagine I became hard to live with in the yard during those months but I gradually came to realise that the guv'nor would not be rushed. My first ride for him came on 8 March 1974. It was on another showpiece course, Sandown Park, but by putting me on an unraced four-year-old called Bilbo, he was not exactly pushing glory into my grasp.

My letter home that week was longer than usual, and more animated. I related how I had left a phone message with a neighbour of my parents', getting her to tell them I would be riding.

> I told them to tell you it's the worst horse in the yard, which we all thought it was. It couldn't even keep up in the gallops at home so I thought I would finish a mile behind, but it wasn't so.
>
> So I jumped him off with the leaders, determined to get a mention on the commentary at the bookies, at least. I was in second and third position for most of the race and towards the end they gradually crept by me. To my surprise I finished eighth of twenty starters. When I came back to the unsaddling paddock, Tom Jones and the owner were delighted ... so Sunday, yesterday, I went in and saw him and asked if he had got any rides for me this week, knowing full well he hadn't, being as it's the big Cheltenham Festival meeting. Anyway, he hummed and hawed for a while and eventually said he hadn't but more than likely next week. So I was just about to leave and he called me back and told me to come and see him every Sunday about 10 a.m. and he and I would sort out the rides, or ride, for me the coming week. So even on my Sundays off I have to go and see him, but the ball's certainly starting to roll now.

Indeed it was. I rode Bilbo again ten days after, this time in more modest company at Wolverhampton. He finished fifth of twenty-two after I had disputed the lead for much of the trip. This time, the letter home was three pages shorter and less bubbly. 'Jones reckoned I made too much use of him,' I reported rather discourteously. Already, I was learning that trainers do not always slap you on the back and buy you a drink when you get beaten.

Tom Jones gave me two more rides before the season ended, both on a five-year-old staying hurdler called Cannelino. In the first of these, I hit the deck for the first time when he slipped up during a four-horse race at Towcester. I wrote indignantly to my folks that the owners of this animal had told me, none too sympathetically, to get some glue on my pants next time. Slightly to my surprise, there was a next time quite quickly, as I kept the ride when Cannelino went to Warwick for a twenty-three runner handicap in May. I got him round this time, albeit unplaced.

So my first season ended. Six rides, no winners. I brooded through the summer, through the season of what I had now disparagingly come to call 'monkey racing'. Only jumping mattered to me now, and the 1974–75 season could not begin too soon. When it did, though, I had a long wait for my first ride, back at Cheltenham on Mackeson weekend again, but my second put me in the winner's enclosure. Ballysilly, trained by Tom Jones, was sent off the 5–1 second favourite for a novice hurdle at Market Rasen on 29 November 1974, and he beat the odds-on shot, ridden by Colin Tinkler, a cosy four lengths. It was not as eventful a ride as my first had been, nor was it the type of race to attract any great publicity. For me, though, it was probably the most important landmark of all. Despite having to travel home in the horsebox, which meant a late-evening return and no opportunity for any celebrating, the smile never left my face. I felt an elation that day which not even the biggest of winners in more recent years could match. These days, while I hope I am far from blasé, I feel that riding winners is my job and if I am not kicking them home pretty regularly I am doing something wrong. In 1974, I had been haunted by the private dread that I might never get to partner a winner at all. Ballysilly was my one off the mark and, like a batsman ending a run of noughts by hitting a four, the relief was indescribable.

For the remainder of that first, full season, my rides were still irregular, thirty-eight in all, of which three won. Tom Jones put me up whenever he could, usually in the apprentice events which were, at the time, called Opportunity races. My outside rides continued to be hard-earned, via the pay-phones, and invariably for the type of trainer who was anything but a household name. One such trainer was Len Carrod, who had a handful of horses somewhere in Lincolnshire. I thought I had hit the jackpot with Len because, when I phoned him to seek the ride on one he had entered for a Saturday meeting at Market Rasen, he said that I could also ride one for him at Sedgefield on the Monday. What is more, he kindly offered to put me up on the Saturday night to save me going all the way back to Newmarket prior to the trek to County Durham.

I am not sure quite what I expected of the Carrod residence. The only trainers' houses I knew were those in Newmarket and, as a rule, they were desirable and extensive properties. So it came as something of shock when Len drove me back after the Market Rasen meeting to a home which consisted of a caravan in a scrubby field. There were four berths, but these were all occupied by family, and my bed for the next two nights was to be a sofa.

It was all part of the learning process, and I was soon streetwise enough to know that very few trainers had the resources which I had come to take for granted at Green Lodge. Fortunately, I had realised very early that a young rider trying to make his way in the game could not afford to be too selective about the people he rode for or the horses he partnered. A quality ride for a known trainer was a rare luxury.

There were times when I felt it necessary to be generous with the facts in order to persuade a trainer I could do the job. I remember picking out the name of Albert Neaves, who trained at Faversham in Kent, and answering his initial question, as to how much I had ridden, quite shamelessly. 'I've had a stack of rides, guv'nor,' I said, 'and a fair few winners.' At the time, the score was one winner and no more than a dozen rides. But, whether he believed me or not, Albert took me on and, for the next two or three seasons, he helped me as much as anyone, putting me up on almost everything he ran.

Albert's instructions in the paddock never altered, no matter the course, the conditions or the quality of the race. 'Jigger me, boy,' he would say, 'just jump out and make all.' His horses were always fit to do their job and, to my initial surprise, some of them did indeed make all and win. His tactics were well known among other jockeys, however, and one day at Lingfield I learned a valuable lesson from the vastly more experienced Paul Kelleway.

We were circling down at the start of this hurdle race when Kelleway came alongside and said he guessed I would want to make the running as usual. When I confirmed this, he said, 'Well, you're not doing it today. I'm going to make it.' This was just the sort of challenge I could never ignore and I had my chest puffed out and my horse's nose pressed up against the tape even before the starter had walked across to his rostrum. I couldn't see Kelleway and when I stole a glance over my shoulder I was surprised to see him out the back. His eyes, though, were fixed on the starter and although I bounced my horse out as soon as the tapes went up, I was dismayed to find Paul five lengths in front before we reached the first flight. He had hit the gate running, always preferable to a standing start, and I am afraid it cost me the race, Kelleway holding me off by a length.

That was an instance of my naivety being exploited but I like to think I learned fast from such episodes. It is also worth recording that I cannot name a single senior jockey who took unfair advantage of me, either in terms of bullying or, except during that strange first ride, straightforward villainy. They did not all go out of their way to be helpful but, now that the roles are reversed, I can well see why. When you have been at the job a good few years and are riding decent horses five or six days a week, the last thing you want is an incompetent boy under your feet. So I was often growled at and told to stay out of the way. I seldom took any notice.

Throughout this time, David Mould continued to be a self-appointed advisor. I had enormous respect for him and welcomed the occasions when he would seek me out after I had ridden a race, asking me how I thought I had done before giving his own constructive opinions of where I might have gone wrong. Race-riding is largely a matter of learning through trial and error but it was still a great benefit to have someone of David's accomplishment to point me the right way.

By the time I was getting going, though, David's career was pretty much over and the job as number-one jockey to Tom Jones had passed to Ian Watkinson. A character for whom the phrase 'larger than life' might have been invented, Ian was the most courageous jockey I have ever known. At times, that courage could have been thought foolhardy but Ian was a man who refused to acknowledge either fear or pain. His career ended in the way, sadly, that was always likely. He had one bad fall too many. A terrible tumble at the final ditch in a Towcester steeplechase left Ian unconscious. He did not come round for several days and, when he did, his memory was muddled. The effects remain with him today, a sad postscript to the sort of career which is the stuff of National Hunt legend.

During our time together with Tom Jones, Ian and I were virtually the only jump jockeys in Newmarket, so it was inevitable that we would have some sort of relationship. We were close friends, no doubt about that, but the nature of the competition which developed between us meant that human emotions, such as jealousy, also came into play. Ian had spent ten hard years in the north before he came to Newmarket, years in which he rode many bad horses and suffered many broken bones. Now, no sooner did he secure one of the better jobs in jump racing than some cocky kid came through the ranks to threaten it. That, in any case, was how I imagined he saw things and it would certainly account for the slight atmosphere which could occasionally undermine our friendship.

Thankfully, the undercurrent was never more than slight. Ian and I had some wonderful times together, sharing a zany sense of humour which others may sometimes have found outrageous, and generally living life from day to day, never worrying about tomorrow.

'Watty' was not made to be a jockey. Tall and big-boned, his weight would balloon above twelve stone in the close-season, which led to an annual ritual of diet, deprivation and discomfort. The first two, he suffered alone but, being his constant driving companion, I had to endure a little of the discomfort. One of Ian's weight-loss devices was to drive in a sweat suit, zipped up to the collar. To increase the effect, he would wind up the car windows and have the heater on its winter maximum. He was doing this as each jump season began, in the balmy holiday weather of early August, and it mattered not a jot to him that his younger passenger had no weight worries whatever. My brief was just to put up with this torture for the common good, and more than once I was obliged to strip down to my underpants as we headed for some west country meeting in Ian's do-it-yourself sauna.

Year after year, he somehow got down to a reasonable riding weight. Year after year, he was in demand and, while the more cautious of our profession will always think twice, and usually say no, when offered the ride on a dodgy novice chaser with three Fs against its name in the form book, Ian would habitually say yes. He was known as the 'Iron Man', and not without excellent reason. But, while we all admired his bravery and resilience, we also winced at the mangling his body took from relentless falls.

Not that he ever spared himself any sympathy. Indeed, he seemed to resent the merest hint that he might ever miss a day's work through injury, and would go to some extraordinary lengths to avoid it. The most extreme example of this dates back to 1976, when he won the Oxo National at Warwick – a four-mile handicap chase, if you please – with a broken leg in a splint. How many painkillers he had taken, I have no idea; how he got past the course doctor is anyone's guess. But Ian was a past master at such things. He fancied his horse, Tom Jones's Jolly's Clump, and he did not intend to let anyone else poach the ride. And, after all, what was a broken leg to him?

If the risks he took brought inevitable penance, Watty did seem to attract bad luck, too. One day at Sedgefield, he took a ride on one of those horses whose continued presence on our racecourses is due entirely to owners and trainers who confuse loyal determination with expensive idiocy. He never had been any good over hurdles, indeed he had seldom jumped a full set, but now, with a fresh burst of misplaced optimism, his connections were sending him novice chasing at the age of twelve. It went without saying that I. Watkinson was their man; it was just as predictable that the partnership should come to grief.

There was a degree of rough justice, however, in that the horse broke down on the flat and Ian, unable to pull him up before the next fence, was catapulted out of the saddle as his crippled mount ploughed into the obstacle. There was then an element of black comedy as Ian, loaded onto a stretcher, was fired 'out of the saddle' for the second time in a few minutes when one of the two ambulancemen tripped up and dropped his handles. The second spill broke Ian's nose. The first had done no more than bruise him.

The ongoing bane of Ian Watkinson's life was dislocating his knees. Anyone who has ever suffered this even once knows how excruciating the pain can be and how bloated and useless the knee becomes afterwards. It happened to Ian several times a season, testing even his powers of resistance. But one day at Wetherby, he not only successfully concealed the pain, he also went out and rode again an hour later.

The incentive was a horse called Tingle Creek, and only for that reason can I understand how and why he did it. I have ridden better horses than Tingle Creek but I have never ridden such an exciting jumper. To partner him for two miles over fences was a thrill unmatched in this job and might even have persuaded others to emulate Ian's heroics. I doubt, however, if they would have succeeded.

Tom Jones was not present at Wetherby that afternoon. If he had been, he might very well have stopped him riding. As it was, Ian had to be helped into the parade ring by the yard's head lad, and virtually lifted onto the back of Tingle Creek. This horse habitually made all; it was the only way he knew how to run. On this day, though, he was no better than second out of the gate and did not take up the running until after jumping the first. He won, as he was expected to do, but at what cost to his jockey was only evident when the indestructible Watkinson had to pull off the A1 on the way back to Newmarket, groggily submitting to the remorseless pain from his knee. He found a phone box and put in a call to Green Lodge, hoping that the guv'nor would come out and pick him up. By now, however, news of the race had filtered back to HQ and before Ian could tell his story, Tom Jones had begun berating him for missing the break and not leading to the first. The phone was banged down and Ian had to hobble back to his car and pilot himself home as best he could.

This incident may seem to show Tom Jones in a poor light; in fact, he was quite unaware that Ian had ridden the horse under such a handicap and, the following day, Ian told me, he received the closest thing to an apology he would ever get from him. The guv'nor was a hard man but essentially a fair man and I can pay him no higher personal compliment than that I would like to think I would still be riding for him now if he had not given up training jumpers. What Ian and I knew we could always expect from Tom Jones was loyalty, a commodity which has fallen sadly into disrepair in many other training yards.

Ian was not pushed out. He could have stayed longer. But, come 1977, he could see the writing on the wall. He might have been riding better horses than at any previous stage of his career but the falls were becoming ever harder to ignore. And, niggling away in the background was this upstart whose company he had, I hope, come to enjoy but whose youth was increasingly being promoted by the yard. Ian took a retainer with Peter Bailey which still ensured him some good horses, and the number-one position with Tom Jones passed to yours truly.

It was to be all too fleeting a privilege. By the end of the 1970s, Tom Jones was almost exclusively a flat-race trainer. It was he who introduced the first Arab owners to the British racing scene and, once he had created such a gravy train, it made simple sense for him to concentrate his interests in that direction. For a year or two, he continued to have a handful of jumpers but then they, too, were moved on, viewed more as a distraction than a value.

Short though it was, however, it was a good time in my life and I count myself fortunate to have ridden some very able horses for him. In 1977–78, we had a novice chaser called Pavement Artist, who picked up the Bobby Renton race at Wetherby en route to one of the most prestigious prizes of the first half of a season, the Hurst Park at Ascot. Back at Ascot, the same season, I won the Long Walk Hurdle on John Cherry. He was at his peak that season and went off at 11–8 favourite. Two years later, one of the jumping remnants in the yard, we were to team up again to win the same race, this time at a less fancied 6–1.

But of all the horses I rode out of Tom Jones's yard, none was more exciting than Tingle Creek and none had such potential as Sweet Joe. Between them, these two horses gave me the greatest moments of my early career and, along with their trainer, they did a great deal to establish me as an ongoing concern in the weighing-room. I still had a long way to go up the pecking order towards that number-one peg, but I was on my way.

From the day when David Mould left the yard, Tingle Creek had always been Ian Watkinson's ride. They were a good pairing and, much as I coveted it, there seemed no chance of the ride coming my way while Ian was in one piece. I had to wait until late in 1977 to take over and, when it came, it was because Peter Bailey had claimed Ian to ride for him at Worcester. Tingle was to run on his beloved Sandown Park and everything was in his favour – firm ground, small fields and a big crowd to adore him. Four years earlier, he had won over the course carrying a big weight and set a new track record. The racecourse later named the event after him, which was fitting. Sandown, with its rapid sequence of fences down the back straight, certainly takes some jumping, but to this horse it always seemed a positive pleasure rather than a problem.

Until that October day, the only occasions when I had so much as sat on Tingle Creek were Sunday mornings, when the exercise consisted literally of taking the horses for a stroll up the lanes. I had never cantered, worked or schooled him, yet I felt I knew what to expect and had absolutely no nerves. I hitched up my irons a notch, sat up his neck and just let him get on with the job.

I don't think I could ride Tingle Creek if he was around nowadays, not because I would be windy but because experience would be telling me I should be organising him. He needed no interference, no real encouragement at all, just a jockey who would flow with him rather than checking his rhythm. His style was simple and exhilarating. He broke fast from the gate and if horses could have a recognisable grin on their faces I swear his would have stretched from ear to ear as he was unleashed towards the first obstacle. The jumping was what he loved. He was fast, brave and as extravagant a leaper as any horse I have ever sat on.

There were only six runners at Sandown that day but Tingle was not favourite, partly because he was giving away weight all round but also because, I tend to think, he was underestimated. The bald form-reading of the race, however, sums up his usual style to perfection. 'Tingle Creek – made all, all out.' He always did make all and he often seemed to be all out. It was just that the others found it so hard to get to him. He was strongly challenged, at and after the last, but he rallied like a tiger up that Sandown hill to win by half-a-length. The roar which greeted us as we came into the winner's enclosure was like nothing I had experienced before and I went out for the next race on cloud nine. I think it showed.

My second ride was also for Tom Jones and, in its way, as fulfilling as the first. There were only four runners for the John Skeaping Hurdle, quite a valuable conditions event, and one of these was a 66–1 no-hoper. I was on Swift Shadow, the oldest horse in the field. I had won on him at Worcester first time out that season, when he easily beat an illustrious odds-on-shot in Grand Canyon, but when that rivalry resumed at Kempton four weeks later, my horse fell at the second flight. He was sent off the 15–2 third favourite at Sandown, and, considering the opposition was headed by two very fine young horses in Dramatist and Birds Nest, that seemed about right.

Dramatist, trained by Fulke Walwyn and ridden by the royal jockey, Bill Smith, had been a close third in a decent race at Newbury on his reappearance, Night Nurse and Beacon Light only just in front. He was a worthy favourite. But my blood was up after Tingle Creek's win and I set out to dictate the race from the front.

It was one of those rare, heady days when everything went to plan. I set a strong early pace, then slowed the race as we went down the back before kicking decisively on the home turn, with two left to jump. Dramatist and Birds Nest were hanging on with a chance at the second last but I had kept a bit of petrol in the reserve tank. Swift Shadow quickened up really well and won by a length-and-a-half.

That weekend, I received more favourable publicity than from all my previous rides put together. That weekend, I felt I had arrived as a jockey. There was more learning to be done, because in truth that never stops, but I felt able to compete on equal terms with the best around. That season was the first in which I rode fifty winners. My final total of fifty-one was a long way behind Jonjo O'Neill's record-breaking 149 but it was good enough to put me up among the top ten in the final jockeys' table. And there, for a decade or more, I was to stay.

I have made much of the contribution made by Tom Jones to this coming of age and I shall always maintain that I could not have made it without him. My impetuous character would, in some way, have led me to self-destruct. But of all the other trainers who helped me clamber up into the first division, Ian Wardle was my most valuable ally. It is strange how we have remained close for so many years when his relationship to me has altered so often – first, a fellow old boy of the same school, then travelling head lad at the same stable, before becoming a successful west country trainer and, latterly, a jockeys' agent. We have had plenty of good times together but those late-seventies years were the best, and I had been literally on the point of accepting a retainer with him when Tom Jones offered me his number-one job. It was on the very day that I had decided to tell the guv'nor I wanted to sign a contract with Ian that he announced my appointment.

I could never have left Tom Jones, though. I had already told Ian that I wanted to continue living in Newmarket, riding for the guv'nor whenever he wanted me. As things transpired, I got the best of both worlds, as our runners seldom coincided with Ian's and I was able to ride most of his, too.

But, for all the winners I was now beginning to ride, the precious few in which I partnered Tingle Creek were the most memorable. On 4 November 1978, back at Sandown Park on the corresponding day to my double of the previous season, he ran for the last time. It was a pre-planned retirement and it could not have turned out better had the whole thing been stage-managed.

It was only right that he should bow out at Sandown, and in the race he had virtually made his own. It was only right that he should go out with a win and, thank heavens, he did. It was asking too much of the old boy, we thought, that he might once again lower his own two-mile track record but, as if he read our untrusting thoughts, he managed that, too.

He won by five lengths, going off the 7–2 second favourite. 'Jumped well, made all, ran on well,' reported the *Sporting Life* formline, which was perfectly accurate but hardly did justice to the passion of the occasion. Their race reporter, Len Thomas, came closer to that when he wrote:

> Not since the days of Arkle have I witnessed an ovation such as that accorded to Tingle Creek at Sandown on Saturday ... It was a real fairy-tale ending. The crowd, sensing victory as Tingle Creek fairly flew the Pond fence, the third from home, urged him on. Their roars reached a crescendo as the old horse, still full of running, fairly pinged the last, leaving the others in his wake.

He was twelve years old but much younger at heart. This was his fifth win at Sandown and his twenty-third in all, but he never won a race at Cheltenham, nor even threatened to. It seemed he hated the place. His fans forgave him readily, though, and on that last day at Sandown they cheered him every step of the path back to the familiar winner's enclosure, to an emotional owner and a misty-eyed trainer.

Tingle Creek was the Desert Orchid of his day. The public adulation was not so strong, partly because he was not a grey and partly because he was not quite as good or as versatile. But the front-running and the bold jumping were comparable and my horse put a fair few on the attendance whenever he ran. He was just on the downgrade by the time my turn came to sit on him but we still enjoyed some great rides together, the films of which sometimes give me a shiver down my spine when I review them now.

Sweet Joe was entirely different. He had more scope in every sense and I believe he could have won me a Gold Cup if he had stayed sound. As a four-year-old, in 1976, he won the Victor Ludorum Hurdle at Haydock, which confirmed him as a quality horse over the smaller obstacles. But jumping fences, over a longer trip, was always going to be his game, and as the 1977–78 season developed, it became clear that there were two outstanding novice chasers in the country. One was Peter Easterby's Alverton, who won the two-mile Arkle Novices Chase at that season's Cheltenham Festival before going up in distance to win the following year's Gold Cup. Alverton died in action, but at least he died in glory, the Gold Cup already won. Sweet Joe never had that chance.

He did, at least, enjoy the fruits of one Festival, though. It was the first winner I had ridden there and, as such, the one I remember more vividly than any other. I had been before, leading up a horse or two for the guv'nor and goggling, open-mouthed, at the scale of the occasion, the volume of people and the passion they create. I knew even then that this was the ultimate, the peak for which everyone in National Hunt racing must strive each year. There was no disappointment when I touched that peak for the first time. It was every bit as good as I had dreamed it might be, if somewhat less comfortable.

Sweet Joe was to run in the Sun Alliance Chase, over three miles, on the first day of the Festival, not only to avoid taking on Alverton – I happened to think our horse would have beaten him, certainly at the longer trip – but because he had already shown that stamina was his forte. He was a genuinely high-quality racehorse and I was naturally excited by the possibility of riding a winner at my first Festival. I was well prepared for it in almost every sense. The mistake I made was in not curbing

Right Tingle Creek.   *Above* My first Cheltenham Festival Winner, Sweet Joe, in March 1978.

Who's a cheeky boy, then!

my youthful enthusiasm enough to take a day off on the Monday before the meeting began.

Then, as now, Southwell stages the pre-Cheltenham meeting. These days, with its financial windfalls from all-weather racing, Southwell is quite a thriving concern. In the late 1970s, there were few more rustic or remote places to ride. I vowed that year that I would never again take a ride at the meeting; like giving up alcohol when in the throes of a hangover, the damage had already been done. I had taken a spare ride in a steeplechase, he had fallen and I had cracked my collarbone.

Human nature dictated that my first thoughts were for myself, for the rides I stood to miss and, especially, Sweet Joe. Then I thought of all the other people, from Tom Jones downwards, who I would be inconveniencing, if not actually letting down. Then I thought of Ian Watkinson and I knew that I was going to ride at Cheltenham, busted collarbone or not.

I had the collarbone strapped to ease some of the pressure. I took copious amounts of painkillers. But I mistimed the tablets and, by the time the Sun Alliance was run, the effect of the last pill was fast wearing off and the pain was a constant, teeth-gritting reminder of my folly.

Sweet Joe won, beating sixteen others, by twenty-five lengths and more, at a generous starting price of 12–1. So much for novice status, I thought. Next year, the big one. Jump racing, however, perennially builds us all up only to knock us flat. Sweet Joe was injured early the following season and never raced again.

Chapter Six

'Friends like Steve Smith Eccles are few and far between ...
we have had enough laughs together to last each other a
lifetime. "You might be dead tomorrow" was our excuse
for doing just about anything and in his case anyone we
knew we shouldn't. We did anything from pretending to
shoot cyclists from the car window with the humane killer
to pinning girls' tights to the coat collars of stewards, while
the other one kept them distracted. Provided it never hurt
anyone's feelings, we were game for anything ... The great
thing about him is that, win, lose or draw, he'd always be
ready to enjoy himself ...'

John Francome, *Born Lucky*

John Francome has been my best friend for years, an eventuality
I would not have believed possible on the day I made his
acquaintance. First impressions were not good. To be blunt, I
considered him a rude bighead.

It was the mid-1970s. I was a young nobody, scratching around
for rides. John was on his way to the first of his jockeys'
championships and it seemed to me that he was all too aware of
it as he barged past me just outside the entrance to a racecourse
one autumn lunchtime. I recognised him immediately, then stood
by while he made a scene at the turnstiles. John had apparently
left his jockey's pass at home and the gateman, true to his breed,
was taking the jobsworth role against him. John gave the wretched
official a mouthful which ended up with words to the effect of,
'Don't you know who I am?'

Classifying him instantly as too conceited for my liking, I made a mental note to stay out of his way, and it was, indeed, only very gradually that I came to know the real John Francome, who has a realistic opinion of his many and varied talents but is as good a friend as anyone could wish to have.

Within five years of that unpromising first encounter, 'Franc' was my choice for best man at my wedding. From that year to this, we have annually gone to Portugal together in the summer. Whenever I am in Lambourn I stay with John and when he comes to Newmarket he stays with me. It is expected, accepted routine and, although nowadays we might go from month to month without seeing each other, the established camaraderie re-ignites the moment we meet up.

The first time I stayed with him, he was still living in the red corrugated-iron house which he had taken on as his first married quarters. The red tin hut, we called it. We didn't know each other very well and when I surfaced the following morning, quite possibly after a good few whiskies in some Lambourn hostelry, I set off for the day's racing leaving my bed unmade. When John arrived at the races he gave me hell, calling me an ungrateful bastard and saying I needn't expect to stay with him again if I was that untidy.

It was a one-sided conversation and I think it is the closest we have come to falling out. John is not everyone's idea of easy-going and he has put up plenty of backs in his time. But, apart from the occasional competitive disagreement over the running of a race, we have never had a cross word. It can be difficult to say why one gets along with one person and not with another, but in the case of John and me, I think it comes down to a shared sense of humour. We both love laughing. Our conversation on a racecourse would seldom be about horses, much more probably about sex, cars or football, and my abiding memory of the years I spent sitting next to him in the weighing-room is that they were fun. John was up to mischief every day and, if some people considered him outrageous and others may have thought the pranks we got up to were childish, they all helped to make up some of the best years of my life. I still enjoy my riding but the weighing-room has never been the same since the day in 1986 when, quite spontaneously, John packed up riding.

John was never likely to plan his retirement in the way most people do. Nor was he likely to wait for the fall which made it obligatory. He had been shaken, more than physically harmed, during the Cheltenham Festival that year when The Reject, a talented but dodgy jumper trained by Fred Winter, came down in the Arkle Chase with one of John's feet trapped in the iron. When The Reject's next outing resulted in another fall, John saw the red light and, true to his nature, marched back into the weighing-room and announced he had ridden his last race. There was no fuss, no emotion – at least, not from him. To tell the truth, he had simply had enough. The daily slog around the nation's steeplechase courses no longer held any fascination for a man who had achieved everything he had set out to do, and more. He might never have won the National, but virtually every other big race had come his way, along with seven jockeys' championships. He would have been tolerably rich through racing alone but John is not a man for tunnel vision. Restless, acquisitive and blessed with being gifted at almost anything to which he turns his agile mind, he is not happy unless he has at least three diverse projects underway simultaneously. In recent years, his public persona has been as an increasingly prominent member of the Channel Four television racing team and as a novelist whose sales have begun to compare with that annual institution, the Dick Francis thriller. But behind the mask, 'Franc' has still been active with horses, riding out for certain trainers, teaching young horses to jump and, on another level, supplying a daily telephone tipping service. As if this was not enough, he spent several years building a lavish new property. Back to his roots, this, as John's father, Norman, is a builder and, in between running fish and chip shops and concocting innumerable other schemes for an overactive life, John has never been shy of pursuing his grand designs with some hard labour. His homes are invariably self-built and I can see he gets great satisfaction from it.

Within a few months of retiring from the saddle, John had embarked on a training career. He had all the facilities ready to hand, having been far-sighted enough to build boxes, and an indoor school, on his own land. He never goes into anything without self-confidence and I imagine he assumed that sufficient owners would be bound to put horses his way, after all the winners he had ridden for the right people down the years. This was his first disappointment. He was sent horses, all right, but not in the numbers, or of the quality he might have expected.

His second setback was a cruel one. 'Franc's' first runner was a horse called Crimson Knight, at an early-season meeting at Worcester. He had got the horse fit, he was well fancied, and I had the ride. He would have won, too, giving my old mate the perfect boost, but after going easily to the front turning into the straight, he went right through the third last and fell heavily. I felt bad enough about this, a sense of irrational guilt depressing me. When I heard that the horse had dropped dead in his box on the racecourse, I was inconsolable.

Paradoxically, I reckon that mishap distressed me more than it did Franc. He had turned up at Worcester carrying his colours in a plastic shopping bag, whistling contentedly and doubtless dreaming up some new money-making scheme even as he went through the motions of being a businesslike trainer. He was in the weighing-room, laughing and joking in the same old way, straight after my fall. I honestly don't know how the horse's death affected him but he has such a capacity for treating triumph and tragedy as frivolities that I would take a bet he lost no sleep.

More than two months passed before Franc had his first training success but it was worth waiting for. It came in a valuable, televised three-year-old hurdle at Sandown. I was on board again as That's Your Lot, an apparent no-hoper at 25–1, romped in by six lengths. The reception in the winners' enclosure showed how much affection the public had for the man and, that day, he did show some genuine emotion. Yet, before the end of that season, it was plain to me that his heart was not really in the training game. He started talking of going round the world for a year, escapism which does not sit easily with the task of building up a competitive yard, and, although circumstances later dictated that he moved house and took a break from training, I don't believe he had any subsequent intention of resuming.

Training, perhaps, did not suit John's make-up. He has never liked being beholden to anyone; even when retained by Fred Winter, the relationship was such that John always had his say and lived his life in the way he chose. Having to deal with the horses and their owners twenty-four hours a day was, I think, anathema to him. It could be said that training was one of the few failures of Francome's life but he probably prefers to think of it as a lucky escape.

Race-riding, by comparison, came ridiculously easily to him. Brought up on showjumping, at which he was a junior international, John came into racing with a natural feel for riding over obstacles. He soon showed he had a clock in his head for assessing the pace of a race, and the years brought him the strength in a finish which, early on, might have been his shortcoming.

There were those who thought Jonjo O'Neill was the greatest and, now, there are plenty who sing the praises of Peter Scudamore. To me, these two fall into a similar category – admirably dedicated riders, way above the ordinary but without that spark of genius which made Francome so special. He is the best jockey I have seen and I do not expect ever to see another to compare. But, like a batsman to whom centuries come as a matter of routine, John was so good at the job that it could bore him.

Give him a challenge and he was inimitable, a master at work. I could watch him riding in a steeplechase on the weighing-room television and know without seeing it that a fence was four strides away, because Franc had an unmistakable method of dipping his body in the saddle to measure the stride and range of each jump. His judgement was usually impeccable and he had the ability to tack right round the outside of the field, sitting motionless and apparently uninterested, only to materialise when it mattered, crouched low and offering some cheeky advice to the toilers he left in his wake as he swept through to win.

But on a rainy day at Fontwell, John could sometimes lose interest in the sport, and it was then that he would begin getting into mischief. He needed excitement and diversions, so he would mess around in a race rather than give it his undivided attention and, between events, he would plague the lives of everyone in authority.

If John had no respect for racing stewards, it was primarily because he knew for a fact that they had no respect for him. The day when a stipendiary steward strode into the weighing-room barking, 'Francome, come with me. The stewards wish to see you,' was the day that things changed for the better. John refused to move from his seat until the 'stipe' addressed him as Mr Francome. From then on, the uncivilised practice of calling jockeys by their surnames alone has been dropped. John, however, did not drop his antipathy to authority. It was an irresistible bait to him; the more pompous the official, the greater the lengths to which John would go to irritate or humiliate. He had few inhibitions and no fear of reprisals.

I have seen him brazenly pin a pair of tights to a steward's back while, apparently accidentally, brushing past him on the way to the parade ring. I have seen him use another pair to silence the weighing room bell at Newbury. And, when half-a-dozen jockeys were called before the stewards on the basis that one of them must be the guilty party, I have stood alongside him while he unzipped his flies and gave Bill Smith, who was standing in front of him with hands behind his back, the fright of his life. He used the same instrument to stir a cup of tea meant for a pedantic clerk of the scales and I have seen him substitute yellow disinfectant squares from a urinal for real lemon drops before offering his bag of sweets to a doorman who happened to be a persistent cadger.

Basic, lavatorial humour, I agree. But with the possible exception of the doorman, it did nobody any harm and gave a lot of us reason to laugh on days when the serious business of racing might have been nothing worth smiling about. This was John's talent, brightening the darkest, most depressing raceday with constant, chirruping banter and wicked gags, so that it seemed inconceivable that he ever worried about anything. He did, of course, and I have occasionally seen him in a very different frame of mind, but he was in his element in the weighing-room and I am sure it was the unique clanship of that daily gathering he must have missed more than anything.

Other than the unavoidable flashpoints which are common to every competitive sport, John was very seldom at odds with another jockey and they, in turn, tended to like and respect him, not only as the flagbearer for their profession but as genuinely good company in the workplace. But his relationships with others in racing were not always so cordial. Franc was opinionated and outspoken, qualities which are unappreciated by those who believe jockeys should be the silent servants of the racing aristocracy. John had no time for this view and none at all for the class structure of the sport. He would be courteous to his owners but he would not, in general, address a duke any differently to a jockeys' valet. They were all simply people to John, and that was something I found very endearing.

While he might attract mild disapproval through this attitude, however, he could outrage by his barely disguised opinion that rules and regulations were only there for him to break. He was so blatant in his disregard for authority that he became a natural target for the stewards who, it often seemed, would summon him on the flimsiest pretext just to teach him that he could never win. In many ways, though, win he did.

Franc was heavy for a jockey and, as the seasons passed, he found the wasting increasingly irksome. He disliked saunas, as I do, and had a healthy enough appetite to make strict dieting a penance. He would do it, because beneath it all he was a professional, but he would still frequently arrive at the races knowing he was a couple of pounds or more heavier than the weight at which he was required to ride.

So, with methods which demanded he must be both deadpan and dexterous, he perfected the art of cheating the scales. Sometimes, he would sit angelically on the scales, his tack arranged to make it look as if his saddle was at the bottom of the pile. In fact, there was no saddle there at all. On the walk back from the race, he would casually dispense with another piece of equipment to ensure he weighed in at the correct weight. He did it all with an openness which astounded me, yet successive clerks of the scales were either oblivious to it or perplexed at how he could pull it off.

Many times, John helped me 'lose' a pound or two on the scales. He would wander through with me to weigh out and, having created some diversion for the clerk, would get his toe under the scales and manipulate it until the correct weight was showing. I once tried to return the favour – but only once. I couldn't keep my foot still and the needle lurched crazily up and down until I had to hold up my hands and pretend, to a stony-faced clerk, that I was just having a bit of fun at John's expense.

One thing Franc was never short of, and that was ideas for making money. He tried, usually in vain, throughout his career to obtain a better commercial deal for all jockeys, but he had his own private deals, some of which were more legitimate than others. He had to come unstuck now and again, of course. The John Banks affair hit him hard and I would not presume to make any judgements on a case I know little about. But in 1982, when John, Peter Scudamore and I ended up in front of the Jockey Club stewards at Portman Square, the 'offence' was so innocent that it had not even occurred to me we were doing anything wrong.

It had, inevitably, been John's idea. The Schweppes Hurdle, now renamed but still one of the hottest handicaps of the jumping year, was about to be run and the three of us, all muckers in the weighing-room, quietly fancied our chances. 'Scu' and I were riding horses for Nick Henderson, while Franc had been booked by Paul Kelleway for Donegal Prince. On paper, I probably had the best chance of the three on Mount Harvard, but there were twenty-seven runners, at least half with appropriate form, and none of us could be anything stronger than optimistic. What John suggested, and we agreed to, was that if any of us did win, he should pay the other two £200 each. It was a pooling of resources, if you like, in the very same way that cricketers and golfers have often pooled winnings from a match, and no different in our minds from two jockeys crossing the last hurdle together, both tailed off, and having a fiver on the first to finish.

The important thing was that it in no way affected our riding. Each of us wanted to win and, once down at the start, I am pretty sure the money never entered our heads. As it turned out, this was one of the most exciting Schweppes hurdles I have known, Scu leading to the second last and then giving way to a trio of horses which included mine and John's. It was a blanket finish, a photo necessary to give the verdict to Donegal Prince, with Mount Harvard a gallant third.

Before we left Newbury that night, John reminded us that we could each expect £200 from him. Nothing more was said, at least by us, but John thought the whole business quite amusing, especially, I gather, as he had fancied his horse rather less than ours. He mentioned the side-bets when he was interviewed on radio and, some weeks later, all three of us were interviewed on the subject and then ordered to Portman Square. An inoffensive bit of sport had gone wrong and I think all of us were a shade apprehensive about our likely fate, the tone of the interrogations by the security men having been rather intimidating. It transpired that we were all banned for the first week of the following season, less of a punishment than the interpretation that some people inevitably put on the affair. My answer to them is that if they bothered to have a look at the finish I rode on Mount

Harvard, and still thought I had carved the race up with John and Scu, they are pretty poor judges.

The Francome I knew, the man I sat next to for years, was not an angel in jockey's clothing. But neither was he a villain. Improbably, he has always had a simple lifestyle, not going out a great deal and seldom drinking. I have occasionally got a few whiskies down him, usually on our August stays at the Palace Hotel in Torquay or on British jockeys' team jaunts abroad, but I can appreciate why he doesn't drink – after a couple, he is just plain silly. He is, too, one of those rare animals who has no need of artificial stimulants. He enjoys himself quite naturally without them.

Many people, myself included, will recall John Francome as the best jockey they have seen. But I will remember him for much more than that – tennis partner, regular landlord, camp comedian and loyal friend. We have been through a bit together but, on the whole, I am very glad I did not take too much offence at his boorish behaviour all those years ago.

Chapter Seven

It was John Francome who unwittingly gave my career its greatest boost by passing up a ride in the 1985 Champion Hurdle. The rest, as they say, is history. But while See You Then became my meal ticket and Cheltenham's hurdling crown briefly became my private preserve, I was really only perpetuating a link with the trainer, Nick Henderson, which predates these events by a good many years. In the fairy godfather way of things which has blessed much of my career, Nick came upon the scene and provided me with life after Tom Jones.

Things could have been difficult for me when my long-time guv'nor finally cut his ties with jump racing to focus full-time on the flat. It was not something which had been sprung upon me, indeed it had been signposted from some years back, but when you have spent the best part of a decade at one yard, too many eggs tend to be in that single basket, creating a bit of a shortage when they hit the ground and break.

By that time, of course, I had been raceriding over jumps for five years, had ridden some good winners and made some good, enduring contacts. Ian Wardle, for instance. Ian had also left Tom Jones, though in his case it was because he fancied setting up as a trainer in his own right. He based himself at Wells, in Somerset, and for a number of years he did pretty well, especially round the west country meetings. I rode most of his horses and had a great time, staying in the village pub, when I went down to ride schooling for him.

But to keep myself in the top half-dozen jockeys, I needed to ride for a first division trainer. Enter Nick Henderson. Nick took out a training licence for the 1978–79 season, which was convenient as this was the year in which Tom Jones' jumpers really began to dwindle. Nick had been assistant to Fred Winter for three years and had ridden with some success as an amateur. He was only in his late twenties and had money behind him, being the son of a merchant banker and Jockey Club member. But although this was a privilege which brought him good owners, and quality horses, Nick has never relied upon such perks. From the start, he was a worker, and I think his main motivation may have been the knowledge that his family had always expected him to go into the City. That he had not done so was to some extent a rebellion, and he probably felt the need to make a success of it.

I had ridden against Nick quite regularly but hardly knew him. My introduction to him as a trainer came through Zongalero, a decent chaser Tom Jones had trained for Sir David Montague. Sir David happened to be a close friend of Nick's father – I think they worked in close proximity in the City – and so, as a gesture of support for the new trainer, he sent him Zongalero. I had ridden him regularly up to that point and it was informally agreed that I would continue to do so when available.

Nick had engaged Bob Davies as his first stable-jockey, so, naturally he rode the pick of the string. Bob was a very able pilot but, to my young eyes, he seemed well into the veteran stage. He was, in fact, no more ancient or past it than I am now, but Bob was a shrewd man with an eye on the future and I think, even then, he was beginning to think of a new career as a racecourse official. The less he rode for Nick, the more the door would open for me, a situation enhanced by the decent output of winners I was producing when I did ride for the yard.

Zongalero was due to run in the 1979 Grand National and, as the day approached, my anticipation grew. This, I thought, could be the day to put me on the map. Somebody up there must have read my presumptuous thoughts and decided it was the moment to take me down a peg or two. It was the year when Monksfield was one of three Irish winners on the first day at Cheltenham and when the Gold Cup was won by a very great Irishman, Jonjo O'Neill, riding Alverton. But there had been nothing for me, at the Festival, to compare with Sweet Joe the previous season and my mind was quickly refocused to Aintree and Zongalero. The weekend before the National, I also had some appetising booked rides at Newbury, and I was looking forward to those when I drove down to Devon for a run-of-the-mill meeting on the Friday.

I had just one ride, for Ian Wardle in the handicap hurdle. Expectation was low. So too, maybe, were my defences. Calamity creeps up when it is least expected; such is the nature of the sting. My hurdler never featured with a chance and I was right out the back coming to the final flight. One of the leaders had evidently ploughed straight through it and a section of the hurdle was flat on the grass, leaving a convenient gap. Call it laziness if you like, but I had a tired horse under me and I saw no point in belabouring him with a jump he had no need to make. I elected to steer him through the gap, and that decision produced the worst and most untimely injury of my career.

Of all the potential ways to take a tumble in this game, this has to be the most bizarre. Far from gratefully accepting my offer of a easy path home, my clumsy horse managed to trip up on the piece of brush which had been knocked out of the flight. As much through surprise as anything, I was unshipped as if from a spacecraft ejector seat. I landed head first and the pain which shot spectacularly up my arm was one of the sharpest tortures this job has ever put me through.

Unless he is utterly incapable of either walking or speaking, no self-respecting jockey, eight days from riding a fancied horse in the National, is going to admit that a fall has given him anything worse than the odd bruise. I told the course doctor that I had twisted my shoulder but felt I should be OK to ride the following day. Had he known I had taken a bang on the head, I would immediately have been signed off. Had he known the actual extent of what I had done, there would have been an ambulance waiting for me.

Back in the weighing-room, the pain began to swamp me. A jockey pal of mine named Jamie Bouchard showed a lot of concern and said he would telephone a physiotherapist in Hungerford who might work on my shoulder later in the evening. Then, as I felt incapable of driving my own car, Jamie put me in his and we set off back up the familiar M5, M4 route from the west country.

I had taken a couple of painkillers but they were obviously not strong enough to cope. We had been on the road no more than half-an-hour when I began to feel sick with the pain. There comes a time when there is no point in prolonging a pretence and I knew, at that stage, that Newbury could be wiped from my schedule. That sort of pain did not disappear in a matter of hours. We cancelled the visit to the physio, partly because I did not think I could bear anyone to touch the injured area and partly because I had an overwhelming desire to get back home and into bed. Jamie lived in Lambourn but, selflessly, drove me all the way to the flat in Newmarket which, by this time, I was sharing with my wife-to-be.

Sleep was elusive, fitful and none too restful. The next morning, I submitted to the proddings of a specialist, posed for the x-ray machine and went awkwardly back to bed. The phone rang some hours later and I was able to tell the inquiring voice on the line that I still felt awful. It was the doctor and he was not remotely surprised to hear it. Neither was I, once he had told me I had broken my neck and that there was an ambulance on its way round to collect me.

It might have been worse, much worse. If the spinal cord itself had been fractured, indeed, it would have been goodbye to all this. Paralysis, life in a wheelchair: the nightmare which every jump jockey has, of necessity, to banish from his mind each time he rides but which, tragically, comes back to a few in horrifying reality.

But, had it been that bad, I would not have been wandering around at home, albeit in such pain. I would not have been able to scrape myself off the deck at Devon, even in the bruised and battered state that I managed it. I would not have ridden again, ever. So, as broken necks go, I was lucky. One vertebra was fractured, two others displaced. I would live. And, the doctor assured me in answer to my first anxious question, I would ride again. But not this season.

So that was it. Season over. All chance of Aintree glory gone. I had a week in which to agonise over the thrill I was to miss, tackling those vast and unique fences, for the very first time, on a fancied horse. And then I had a few bewildering minutes to watch someone else do it in my place.

I was living in a flat by that time, in Newmarket's St Mary's Square. Ian Watkinson lived nearby and, although he too would dearly have loved to be riding the fairground attractions of Aintree, it was no great surprise that he was, instead, grinding his teeth alongside me in the front room as David Coleman slickly ran through the preliminaries in front of the massed television cameras. Ian was on crutches, I had my neck propped uncomfortably in a brace. We must have been quite a sight.

Zongalero went off at 20–1 and was well fancied by everyone connected with him. Certainly by me. But as I watched him jump off, under lucky old Bob Davies, and heard the roar from the imposingly ancient Aintree stands, I found myself with a dilemma. All winter long, I had dreamed of making my first National ride a triumphant one on this horse. He was my ride, we got along well together and, as much as jockeys ever do develop relationships with the horses which are such transient companions, I liked him a lot. But now that he was, temporarily, someone else's ride, did that mean I liked him any the less, wished him well less sincerely? In short, did I cheer him on, or did I bury my head in my hands and hope, if a shade guiltily, that he would reserve the glory for another year?

It is difficult to describe my feelings or to assess which emotion, loyalty or selfishness, came out on top. I rode the course with the horse, I know that, and as he jumped the last fence upsides Rubstic, then duelled with him throughout the long, punishing run-in, I felt I was somehow part of the scene, a scene I had played over in my mind time and again in eager anticipation of the race.

As it turned out, perhaps I had the best of all compromises. Zongalero had run heroically but was not quite good enough. Rubstic held him off by a length-and-a-half. I rose from my chair, almost as drained as if I myself had done the riding, and poured a scotch with the consoling thought that we, the horse and I, would go one better next year.

It didn't happen, of course. Such long-term plans so rarely do come to fruition in this fickle game of ours. Twelve months on, we did indeed get horse and rider to the race, fit and well, and we arrived in the glare of publicity which, season after season, accompanies the ante-post favourite for the National. I lapped it all up, savouring the attention. It did not last.

We were deposed as favourites before the off, that honour passing to Rubstic. But he got no farther than the fifteenth; we survived four more fences before, a shade ignominiously, Zongalero and I were credited with a refusal at the twentieth. In truth, it had been on the cards for about a mile. Zongalero had class, and he could jump, but his problem, I had now discovered, was that he was gutless. On his first time round Aintree, he may have jumped well out of fright. Going back was different. He knew what to expect and, depressingly, he did not like it one bit. He was good enough as we hunted round on the first circuit but, when the pace quickened, he began to apply the brakes. He tried to refuse at the nineteenth but I got him over; at the next, his will prevailed.

So the broken neck had, after all, robbed me of my best winning chance on the horse. I regretted that and yet, paradoxically, I did not regret the time that injury gave me. It was too much time, in the normal, hectic way of things, but, immobilised as I was, I fell to pondering on how I had ended up as I was, and how much worse it might have been. Morbid thoughts, maybe, but useful ones, too. It changed me in a significant and lasting way. There was no thought of giving up and seeking a more sensible job – after all, what on earth could I have done which was half as rewarding? – but it did seem appropriate to me that my companion, for that confusing Grand National, had been my dear, damaged friend, Ian Watkinson. I think, in the weeks which followed, I accepted that the Watkinson route, of taking all offered rides and giving them everything for death or glory, was not for me. I was well aware that the accident had been a freak and had no special bearing on the quality of the animal involved. But, as I said, I had time to think.

I wanted to ride good horses, not chase around the country after other people's scraps. I had done my time and had my fill of that. I felt I was ready for a step into the rarefied atmosphere inhabited by the likes of Francome and O'Neill. Great guys both, and I begrudged them nothing. But I envied them, and wanted to be up there with them. I was lucky. Before the start of the 1979–80 jumps season, Nick Henderson asked me down to his home. There, in Windsor House, the unmissable bright yellow building as you descend Hungerford Hill into Lambourn, Nick offered me the job which, one way and another, was to be the passport to the biggest winners of my career. It was not an offer I needed time to contemplate.

Bob Davies was to concentrate on riding for David Morley, who is ironically based on my patch, near Newmarket. For Bob, it was another gentle step towards retirement. For me, the merry-go-round had just begun and my first contracted job since apprenticeship was without question an enviable one. True, Nick had only been training for one season, but it had been a season rich in promise. If the fruits were now ripe for picking, I was a very fortunate man.

It felt that way, too, on my early visits to the Henderson household. Nick is an educated, civilised and urbane man. He mixes in good circles and has a lovely family. I got on well from the start with Diana, his wife. They all made a fuss of me whenever I came down. I liked that because it made me feel important, a feeling every ambitious twenty-four-year-old craves. I wanted to keep things that way and, perhaps, it was for that reason that I decided I would not take the option of moving down to the Lambourn area.

I had dropped roots in Newmarket. I had a lot of friends there, I knew my way around the place, and I was about to buy my first house, in a neighbouring village, to start married life. Di, my intended, had no wish to move to Berkshire and I could see no good purpose behind the inevitable upheaval. So I stayed put and, purely in terms of my future relationship with Nick Henderson, that was an error.

It was not that things went badly. Our first season together was a great success. Nick did not have the number, or quality of horses he was to enjoy in later seasons but he had some very useful animals and, in general, they won in their turn. He built on the promise of his first season and I consolidated a place among the leading half-dozen jockeys. I was in the runners-up position in the table for a good part of the campaign and, but for breaking my collarbone twice – first at Christmas and then, maddeningly, just before Cheltenham – I might have given Jonjo a run for the title.

I was at my peak, twenty-five years old and in demand around the country. There had been a time when I considered going up north, where the jockey competition is less intense, and there had even been a possibility of going to Arthur Stephenson as stable-jockey. But I am not sure Arthur and I would ever have been on the same wavelength and, the way things were as a new decade dawned, I was mighty glad nothing had come of it.

I did not see the danger signs. At least, I did not recognise them. Like a complacent husband who fails to see that his disillusioned wife is having an affair, I jogged happily along in my cavalier style, content in the belief that all was well in my world. But in Nick Henderson's eyes, all was not well. And his were the eyes which mattered.

The virus, that elusive, indeterminate plague of racehorse and trainer, was rampant in Lambourn during the 1980–81 season. Some yards were virtually shut down, incapacitated by the grip of this disease which can lurk unseen in a yard, showing itself only when it is too late, when a horse which had seemed fit and bursting with health runs unaccountably badly. And then the same happens to another and another until the trainer is scared to run any more, no matter how well they seem at home. It is a recurring nightmare for every trainer; it leaves them helpless and frustrated and, in some cases, justifiably ill-tempered.

Nick Henderson had a bad season. If it was not the virus, it was that other bane of the jumping trainer's life, leg problems. The legs of a racehorse are like china; study their spindly design and it is remarkable that any stand up to the rigours of galloping, let alone jumping. But many do not, of course, and sod's law determines that, when a stable is struggling, the injuries pile up.

All trainers live on their nerves, to some extent. It is hard to blame them. The horses in their care are precious, if not all in terms of great value then certainly in terms of their owners' investment. The responsibility is great, the hours endless and the demands punishing. The odd trainer takes it in his stride but Nick is not like that. He is by nature a worrier and, because he is also so very conscientious, he seldom switches off from the job at all.

In his study at Windsor House, Nick kept the clues to his chemistry. There was a Rubic's Cube, a crib set and an ornamental snakes-and-ladders board. He would fiddle with all of them in turn, never in my view finishing a game nor even concentrating on it. These were simply diversions for restless hands while his ever-active brain focused on the diverse problems out in the yard, the fitness of certain horses, tomorrow's runners, riding arrangements, owners who were slow to pay or quick to complain. Such problems were not exclusive to N.J. Henderson, they were and remain the scourge of all training establishments. But Nick took every one of them personally and lived the job to an extreme that put worry-lines prematurely on his face.

He could be sociable when the time was right. I went on holiday with him to Barbados, in those early days, and he was a different person in that environment, a few thousand miles out of Lambourn and a few weeks out of season. But put him back in the business arena and you had a man dedicated almost to the point of obsession.

Nick's nerves were never so nakedly on display as before a big race. He would chainsmoke, but the sought-after comfort never came. I remember walking into the parade ring at Cheltenham before See You Then's second Champion Hurdle and seeing Nick trying desperately to get a cigarette to his mouth with a hand which refused to stop shaking. It probably didn't help matters but I couldn't help laughing as I said, 'It's a bloody good job you're not riding him, boss.'

In that one trivial incident was encapsulated the difference between us, the reason why we could like each other as people but never really gelled as working partners. It was a personality clash, simple as that. Nick was, at the time, a very stressed person. In trying to fulfil other people's expectations of him, and his own punishing demands on himself, he created a pressure cooker inside his head. It found its release in flashes of temper and I, as the man paid to ride the horses, often found myself the target.

It would be quite wrong to suggest he picked on me for the sake of it, or even to deflect pressure or blame. Like most trainer-jockey pairings, we had our disagreements over how horses should be ridden and there were days when he bluntly told me I had ridden a bad race, and he was right. Equally, though, there were days when I knew for certain I had given a horse every chance of winning, and he had simply not been good enough. On days such as that, a trainer's forked tongue is more an expression of frustration than a realistic finger of accusation.

Nick was never very equable in the face of defeat. Not at first, anyway. He did not have to say anything when I came back on a fancied horse which had been beaten. I could tell from the set of his face how he felt, and I knew that there would be no calm and logical assessments done until he was back home and had watched the race on the video. It barely mattered what I said.

But the racecourse was not a place for us to fall out and, apart from the occasional grumpy word from one or other of us, we never did. It was on the schooling grounds in Lambourn that our working relationship deteriorated and eventually, perhaps, where it came to grief.

The root of the problem was the infrequency, even the uncertainty, of my attendance. It was, I now see, a vicious circle. It was because he was such a worrier that I did not want to be at his beck and call at all hours of the day and night, why I had opted to continue living in Newmarket. But it was also because he was a worrier that he wanted me at the yard more often than I was able or prepared to be there. I arranged each week to travel over for a schooling session. For Nick, that was not enough. With his fretful nature and his constant need to discuss and dissect the horses, his ideal was a jockey who would be there three or four times a week.

The journey from Newmarket to Lambourn is not a good one and, on midwinter mornings at dawn, it can be positively evil. There were days when the fog was bad, or East Anglia was iced up, and I didn't make it. Nick would be rightly upset. The distance between us became an increasingly large barrier to good relations and the fact that I was there so seldom merely added to the strain when I was ... Schooling, however, was something in which I took a particular pride. I believe I was well taught during my years with Tom Jones and ever since then I have found great job satisfaction in teaching young horses to jump. I do feel, however, that there is a right and a wrong way of schooling horses and, in this, I was at odds with my guv'nor more than once.

My pet hate, on going into the parade ring to ride a young horse for the first time, is to be told that he schools brilliantly, 'always standing off'. My view is that it is the easiest thing in the world to take a novice onto the schooling grounds in isolation and make him stand off, always going for the long stride. All you are achieving is a false sense of security. It is obviously impossible to accurately simulate race conditions when schooling, but a horse will learn far more if he is first allowed to make mistakes by getting too close and 'fiddling' a fence or two. Once he has done that a few times, he will have a better chance of getting himself out of trouble when, in the inevitable hurly-burly of a novice chase, he can't go long because one has cut across in front of him, or because he misjudges it, or because he is simply tired.

Nick, however, aligned himself with the other school of thought and believed it best to get a horse jumping immaculately from the outset. Whenever one I was schooling made a mistake, I felt he was having a dig at me for failing to put him right, not seeing that this was actually my preferred method. We discussed our differences often enough but still the divide remained, and more than once, tempers flared.

This, it has to be said, was not an unusual occurrence on the Lambourn gallops. They have traditionally been used by most of the trainers in the village, and anyone in racing will tell you that trainers are invariably on a short fuse early in the morning. John Francome tells some tales of Fred Winter's explosions on the gallops and I have lost count of the other incidents I have witnessed, and stories I have heard, relating to one grouchy trainer or other. So Nick and I had not exactly cornered the market when it came to shouting matches. With that said, however, things did happen which I lived to regret.

The worst instance virtually brought our partnership to a close. Both of us were particularly bad-tempered that morning and I was growing increasingly irritated as Nick bawled out his lads. When he transferred his dark mood to me, something snapped. It was the usual subject, an argument about how best a certain horse should be taught. This time, I had had enough. I jumped off and told Nick in no uncertain terms that if he felt that way, he would be better off schooling the horse himself. His reply was equally aggressive and I am afraid, in the heat of the moment, I swung a punch at him.

The only reason I missed was that the horse I was holding took fright at this sudden violent movement and threw back his head, carrying my fist way off target. It was just as well. We glared at each other for a moment or two, then I handed him the reins and marched off to my car.

It was not quite the end, but it might as well have been. It had been a difficult season for Nick and he had been a hard man to get along with. That does not condone what I did, because swinging a punch at the boss was not designed to make for good relations, but it helps explain why the dream team, we pair of young and thrustingly ambitious men, as we were frequently described in the press, broke up at the end of that second season together. We enjoyed each other's company socially – I often went to his house for dinner parties with the owners – but our personalities grated.

If I can find fault with Nick, I have no doubt he was warranted in finding fault with me. Nick cares deeply and transparently about every aspect of his yard, every horse, every runner, every piece of work. My make-up is such that I don't appear to care a damn. He could not cope with that, much less appreciate it. Looking back, I can see that it might have worked better, and for longer, if I had learned the art I now preach to any young jockey making his way – the art of diplomacy. But in those heady days, I scarcely knew the meaning of the word.

It would be an exaggeration to say Nick and I parted on the best of terms. Because there had been an element of acrimony involved, the papers made much of it. But I have never been one to harbour dark thoughts or to bear grudges and neither has Nick. We were to link up again much sooner than either of us could have anticipated but, in the meantime, my penchant for falling out of one job and into another was looking after me once more.

Alan Jarvis was one of the trainers who kept me ticking over with rides, and winners, when my main provider dried up. He had always been small-time, based in unfashionable racing country near Coventry with a small string. But he both trained them and placed them skilfully and, in the summer of 1981, he shifted his operation east to Royston, twenty-five minutes out of Newmarket. I noted this with interest, but not half as much interest as I showed when Alan contacted me to offer a retainer.

I was not seeking another retainer. The memory of how and why I split with Nick was still sharp and, moreover, I was quietly looking forward to being my own master, taking the rides I wanted without deference to a boss. But this was no ordinary retainer, no ordinary job. Alan Jarvis was offering me £10,000 for the season. To put it in context, this was a few thousand pounds more than John Francome ever received from Fred Winter. In National Hunt terms it was a small fortune and, as news of the offer spread, and rumour turned to fact, it caused something of a stir.

I accepted. Of course I did. This was the original offer I could not refuse. But, before half the season was done, the contract had been cancelled by mutual, if unspoken consent.

Alan had moved into King's Ride, a brand new, custom-built yard. The facilities were impressive and Alan evidently felt under pressure to produce some realistic returns. The trouble was, he had thirty horses which, with few exceptions, were not of the standard needed to match the facilities and elevate him into the top flight of trainers. He had a dozen early runners, almost all of which performed moderately, and it was not long before he latched onto the easiest scapegoat, the jockey.

He told me I was riding badly. This seemed at odds with the number of winners I was riding for other trainers. I told him I could not go without the horse. We agreed to disagree. After a time, I stopped phoning him, he stopped phoning me and the arrangement ceased to be. It was like a brief flirtation, put to rest once the early passion was spent. There was no great final scene, no angry words, just a tacit acceptance that it had not worked.

I think Alan is a lovely guy. Others, I know, regard him as looking shifty, but I can only speak as I find. He was straight and generous when I rode for him then, and it has been the same in later years. As with Nick Henderson, there was no lasting ill feeling. Some years on, I began to partner Kathies Lad, the best chaser Alan ever trained. He won the Captain Morgan Chase on Grand National day, two years in succession, the first time only three weeks after winning a tough handicap at the Cheltenham Festival.

Alan Jarvis could train all right, and I would like things to have worked out better between us. But I did not exactly lose on the deal. My retainer was to be paid in two instalments, the first of which I received at the start of the season. Half-a-dozen days of schooling, and maybe twenty rides, seems a good exchange for £5,000.

Chapter Eight

'It takes more than a kick to keep Steve Smith Eccles down...'

George Ennor, *Sporting Life*, 1982

The longer I have been at this game, the more convinced I have become that, at heart, I am a loner. In life, as well as in racing my partnerships have usually had painful endings, leading me to the conclusion that I have always had the freelance spirit. Wherever I hang my hat, that's my home ... someone sang that, and it could be my motto.

There had been any number of kicks to the Eccles ego in the early 1980s. There was the split with Nicky Henderson, then the failure of my lucrative deal with Alan Jarvis. On top of all that was a failed marriage.

If I say that none of these things caused me any enduring regret or depression I will probably, in the last instance at least, sound callous. But the truth is that my marriage to Di Walton had been an ill-fated arrangement, the formalising of a relationship which had perhaps run its best days before we signed the wedding book. Sad though it is when any marriage hits the rocks, I do not think it came as a great shock to either of us.

Living together, in our rented flat, had been fine. After a few years of roughing it in squalid digs, there was a luxurious comfort in having someone to come home to, someone to cook supper and to keep the place, our place, tidy and homely. Sexist, I know, but that is me, I am afraid, and for a couple of years things worked well on that basis. But my banter with my best man, John Francome, about ducking out of the wedding ceremony, had been only half in jest. By then I did have genuine doubts about my commitment to this change of life.

The doubts came home to roost and it was a little under twelve months later that the marriage ended in all but name. We were at a party, given by Tony Ives, a flat-race jockey also based in Newmarket. Di had gone up to the loo and I was standing at the foot of the stairs drink in hand, putting the world to rights with a couple of mates. The discussion settled upon the place of women in our lives, as so often it will when men are left alone, and with a scoff which told of recent squabbling, I said, 'Getting married was the worst day's work I ever did.' My voice is of the stentorian sort which carries above normal conversation, and Di, descending the stairs unnoticed, heard every word of this condemnation.

Given time, I might have tried to explain it away as meaningless men's talk, flippancy without feeling. But I had no time to think. Without a word, Di smacked me round the face and left. I had asked for that much, I suppose, but as she also had the car keys with her she was able to drive my car home, take her belongings and all our ready cash from the flat, and leave for good.

There was a sense of disorientation for a while, but no sense of emotional loss. We were better off without each other. With no children to complicate affairs, we divorced in our own time and resumed an amiable, if remote friendship which still endures now.

Released from even the pretence of monogamy, I had a few wild years. I was in my mid-twenties, very fit and tolerably well known. I had a house of my own, a fast car to drive and a reasonable amount of money in my pocket. I might not exactly have been what a girl's mother would consider a good catch, but I had enough going for me to make the oldest bachelor pursuit pleasurable and rewarding.

More than once, I took liberties with a girl's affections. Sometimes, I got away with it through a talent for glib persuasion. Once, on a not untypical foray in Torquay, I got a headache and an embarrassing scene for my sins.

Devon was traditionally a happy hunting ground for me. I still love the early-season circuit, at Newton Abbot and the course at

Haldon now known simply as Exeter, and make a habit of staying down for a week or so at the Palace Hotel in Torquay. I have stopped there for years and the staff all know me and look after me royally. On the day in question, however, I guess they all had a good laugh at my expense.

The local race clubs generally stage a Start of Season Ball in the area, early in August, and as I was down for the week, I decided to go. I arranged to take a girl called Alex and all would have been well if, halfway through the evening and with a drink or two on board, I had not sensed that I was being eyed up by another, very attractive young lady. Unforgivable it might have been but chivalry gave way to vanity. I returned the look and, in the course of a dance and a discreet drink, arranged to slip away from the hall with companion number two, leaving poor Alex in the lurch.

It was a particularly ungentlemanly thing to do, pure lust getting the better of me, and I did not deserve to get away with it. For the rest of a very pleasant night, however, I did, and it was only the next morning that I had to face the music. Alex phoned through to my room at the Palace. She was in the foyer and she wished to see me.

I went down with a lot of flimsy excuses in my head, knowing that a plea of innocence was out of the question but confident that I might at least make my peace with her. I was wrong, very wrong.

Alex was not alone. She was accompanied by an older woman who, it later transpired, must have been her mother. An aggrieved mother, roused by this man who had wronged her daughter. I ignored her at first, and that was my mistake. Concentrating my attentions on Alex, desperately trying to summon the charm and the plausibility to appease her, I quickly saw that I was getting nowhere. She called me a lot of well-chosen names before preparing to take a swing at me with her handbag. As I reached out to hold her arms down in self-defence, I was felled by a ferocious blow from behind. Mother had hit the jackpot with her bag, and by the feel of it she had packed it with something very solid, malice aforethought.

The fracas found its way into the local paper, which gave everyone in the weighing-room a giggle as well, but in those days such notoriety tended to follow me around. And, while I would have preferred to do without the headache that bag left me, there were times when I might have revelled in the Errol Flynn image.

Sailing close to the wind was part of the game, part of the fun. I remember one night at the Fosse Manor Hotel in Stow-on-the-Wold, a regular retreat for some of the racing fraternity during Cheltenham meetings. I was still technically married and the girl I linked up with was about to be married to a prominent trainer. Caution cast firmly to the winds, we managed to borrow a friend's cottage in the vicinity and spent a very cosy night. The cold light of dawn often brings the first trace of panic, however, and the knowledge that I had been expected back in Newmarket the previous night gave an unusual haste to my dressing. It seemed, for whatever reason, that some of my clothes had been discarded in a hurry and, despite an anxious search, I had to set off for home without my underpants. The lady in question found them, though, and a few days later a mysterious package arrived through the post.

I was formally back in bachelor state when I took out the daughter of a revered Lambourn trainer. We had been friends for a time, but nothing had come of it, so it was a not unpleasant surprise to me when, on this occasion, dinner led to liqueurs, liqueurs led to a nightcap back at her place and the nightcap led us to bed. There was a complication. She lived at home and father and mother would not have been overjoyed to find a rampant jockey in their girl's bed. We made the most of the size of the place and all went well until I had to get up for a pee.

I was given directions, and I don't think there was a sense of mischief attached to them, but the fact is that I blundered straight into the master bedroom where famous trainer and wife were asleep. I was stark naked, half-drunk and it was about three in the morning. I could hardly say I had just dropped by for a social call. Thankfully they must have been heavy sleepers and, heart pounding, I managed to make my grateful escape.

These were three escapades which really did happen. There were others, too, though nowhere near as many as gossip would have you believe. If I had led my social life in quite the daredevil way it has often been painted by racing gossip, I would have been burned out years ago. The true stories are always the best ones, though, and I know they gave endless amusement to John Francome. We often used to share a room in Torquay and we had some great laughs together, but it was a standing joke between us that I would always comb my hair in front of the mirror before we went out and then say, full of smug self-satisfaction, 'I bet you wish you were as good-looking as me.'

John was, and still is, my best friend. But he was also the perennial stumbling block to my career. I never thought of it in any resentful way but it is a fact that I spent the best years of my career in his shadow. While Francome was riding, I had next to no chance of being champion jockey. And then, no sooner was he gone than the next phenomenon came along in the shape of Peter Scudamore. My path was blocked once more.

Scu is now a close mate and a business partner but in his early riding days he was as unlike Francome as can be imagined. John presided over the weighing-room with his incessant banter and his infectious humour. Something was always afoot. Peter sat quietly in the corner with his deep thoughts and intense ambitions.

Because he did not make his presence felt in the weighing-room, I hardly noticed how he rode in his early, amateur days. He was polite and well-spoken but very withdrawn. Franc would forever be telling him to cheer up, but the solemn face, pale and sometimes drawn, did not mean Scu was unhappy. In his own way, which is a remarkably dedicated way, he was simply plotting his path to the top, where he would first challenge and then succeed Francome as the undisputed champion.

In the early eighties, there was another great guy and very fine jockey around. He, too, suffered from sharing an era with Francome but, unlike me, Jonjo O'Neill did win the championship. He also won countless friends with his personality, and I am proud to count myself among them.

Our styles as jockeys were often compared around that time. Jonjo was cock of the north but our paths would cross at the Midlands tracks, and when there was a big Saturday card, and I soon came to know that the kind and gentlemanly Jonjo of the weighing-room was transformed once he got out on the course.

Jonjo was granite-hard in a race, no quarter asked or given, but his greatest quality was never knowing when he was beaten. Many was the time I saw him hard at work, out the back and with apparently no chance, only for his horse to inexplicably respond to the urgings and come charging through with a decisive late run. There was none of the easy, natural grace of Francome about Jonjo's riding, he was a terrier in the style of Willie Carson. But I do not think I have ever seen a more consistently effective rider, nor a braver one. He seemed to be continually fighting back from serious injury and it was the cruellest injustice that, having given so much pleasure and reached the end of a roller-coaster career with body and mind intact, he should be struck down by cancer. I remember feeling sick at heart the day I found out, but I never doubted that Jonjo would win that battle, too.

They may have been very different types of riders, but Francome and O'Neill had one thing in common. They were both close to teetotal during their days in the saddle, no company for me on my increasingly lonely treks to the racecourse bar at the end of a day's sport. Neither, however, needed a drink to enjoy himself and I discovered with some amusement that Jonjo, too, was incapable of holding a drink on the odd occasions he did indulge.

During a jockeys' trip to Limerick races a few years back, someone spiked Jonjo's orange juice. Two glasses, and he was as silly as a six-year-old. He must quietly have enjoyed the experience, though, because when we went to America in 1984, the first foreign venture by a British jockeys' team, Jonjo got stuck into the bourbon on the plane. He came up smiling from that one, too.

One of the things I have always relished in this job is riding up north. The opportunity does not arise as often as I would like, because there is a very distinct north-south divide and a southern jockey is unlikely to pick up spare rides from trainers based north of Nottingham. But my trainers, down the years, have run the occasional one at Haydock or Wetherby and then there has been the odd jaunt to the likes of Sedgefield or Hexham, minor courses where any shortcomings in facilities are more than compensated for by the warmth of the welcome.

Jonjo was a god in these places during his riding days but the northern circuit always has its share of characters, from big Ron Barry through Colin 'Jack' Hawkins and Chris 'Rambo' Grant. Nice guys, all of them, and it was noticeable to me whenever I rode on their patch that they tended to look after each other much more than we do down south.

This is not meant to be patronising. These fellows are as tough as they come. Jonjo and Ron, for instance, are the best of mates but you would not always have known it to see them scrapping in a finish. But the northern scene is certainly less competitive, in that ten or a dozen established jockeys have their acknowledged rides and there are far fewer freelances chasing spares than in the south. This makes for less backstabbing and a more accommodating outlook at the start of a race. Down south, there might be half a dozen young thrusters anxious to make the running and make a name for themselves in a novice hurdle. A similar race in the north is likely to be run at a more sensible, sedate pace, building up slowly to the business end rather than going hell for leather from the moment the tapes rise.

I don't know whether I would have enjoyed being a permanent part of the northern scene, or if I would eventually have missed the brighter lights and faster pace of life to which I have become accustomed. But there was a time, in the late seventies, when it was a serious prospect. Tom Jones was winding down his jumping string and, showing a touching concern for my future, he spoke to Arthur Stephenson to see if he might take me on a retained basis. It came to nothing because I preferred to hitch myself to the southern star of Nicky Henderson. For all the ups and downs of that relationship, I maintain it was the right thing for me to have done. I don't think Arthur and I would have tolerated each other for more than a week. There has been no more consistent trainer than W.A. Stephenson over the years and, right up to his death in 1992, he was churning out winners by the score from his unprepossessing yard in Bishop Auckland. But Arthur, from what I know and hear, was reactionary, reclusive and taciturn. He was all the things I am not, and I fear the clash would have been severe.

There were other jobs on offer around this time. I had begun to ride quite a few for Captain Tim Forster, and with some success. His stable jockey, Graham Thorner, had been obliged to retire, basically after taking too much punishment from heavy falls, and there was a vacancy for which many a jockey would have given much. The Captain is a very traditional type of National Hunt trainer, concentrating on jumping-bred types who are never likely to be much good until they go novice chasing. He has a well-chronicled disdain for flashy hurdling types and I think it was this which deterred me from throwing in my lot with him. I was a pushy young man and I wanted to go places quickly. I thought I had more chance of doing so with Nick Henderson than with Tim.

For some years afterwards, I went on riding some of Tim's decent chasers, whenever asked, and I have always found him an absolute gentleman to work with. But, being the way I am, I suppose my ideal trainer is someone with whom I can have a laugh and a joke. David Nicholson fitted the bill, and so too did Jeff King.

'Duke' Nicholson earned his nickname through some arrogant mannerisms, but he and I know better. Beneath the thin public front, there is a great sense of fun. There has never been any point in anyone talking down to me, because I don't wear it and, although I am content to show the accepted respect to a trainer on a racecourse, I like to feel on equal terms with him in the yard, on the gallops or in the bar. David has always respected that view and we have had some good times together. He is a very social creature but also a highly professional trainer. In his new yard in the Cotswolds, the sky may well be the limit, but he has tasted plenty of success down the years and for the two seasons I was with him, retained as back-up to Peter Scudamore, there were plenty of winners, including one winning appearance on that fine hurdler, Broadsword.

One morning on David's gallops at Condicote, Scu and I schooled forty horses. It was the most hectic, and most fulfilling morning's work I have ever done in racing and the slick way in which the 'Duke' kept producing the horses, as if off a conveyor belt, was impressive to witness.

Like many a trainer, however, David is not always at his best early in the morning and I recall another schooling day when things did not go to plan, largely due to the predatory presence of a hot air balloon, hanging low over the gallops and, predictably, spooking the horses. To make matters even more provocative, the pilot of this contraption was leaning out of his basket and waving as if he had chanced upon a bunch of admiring tourists. David, who may or may not have been suffering from a mild hangover, was not amused. His face was contorted with rage as he glared up at the miscreant. Now, David is a tall and imposing man and presents a formidable opponent when standing his ground to argue a point. Here, however, he was disadvantaged by the 100 feet or so up to the balloon. As if to counter this, he stood up to his full height, in the irons of his hack, jabbed his fingers idiosyncratically at the still waving imbecile, and roared, 'Why don't you bugger off and find some work to do!'

There are those, I know, who find David's manner overbearing, but I believe you get as good as you give. He is generous, kind and a fun-lover, which is good enough for me, and I shall forever cherish the memory of our journey back from a British jockeys' trip to Ireland when David, blazered and tie'd in official team manager uniform, descended the elevator at Birmingham airport sitting in a baggage trolley.

Jeff King was a giant of the weighing-room when I began riding. Any number of old-timers still tell me he was the best around and, although he was never champion, nor did he win the biggest of races, I rode against him enough times to take their point. If I admired Jeff's riding, I also admired his lifestyle. However the day's racing had turned out, Jeff would be ready to buy drinks in the bar, and probably to stop for a couple more and a bite to eat on the road back from a faraway meeting. He worked hard, for there were few tougher or more genuine riders, but he also played hard. This was a philosophy I followed faithfully and willingly, and it may have been because he saw in me a kindred spirit that Jeff and I always got along well and, when he started training in 1981, why he put me up on a lot of his horses.

Jeff had two problems in his early years of training. One was the simple fact that his horses were moderate, in the main bought cheaply for owners who were as much friends as anything. The other was that his judgement of a jockey's performance was unfairly harsh. Jeff expected everyone to ride as well as he had done, which was patently impossible, and when a jockey fell below those demanding standards, he heard about it in Kingy's inimitably blunt terms.

So we had our bust-ups – disagreements over how I had ridden a horse which might become acrimonious. Almost always, though, we would sort it out and forget it over a glass of something in the bar. Argue though we might, Jeff kept using me and I kept going back for more. In the spring of 1984 I helped put him on the map by riding him a winner at the Liverpool National meeting and, the following year, his horses improved and so did our fortunes together. A hurdler called Joy Ride ran four times and won three; his only defeat, and a close one, was at the hands of a horse called See You Then.

My winners came from far and wide during those freelance years, and I struck up some good, lasting partnerships with horses such as Duke of Milan, for Nick Gaselee, and Far Bridge, a talented but difficult horse of Toby Balding's on whom no one else seemed able to win.

In an entrepreneurial spirit, I had various small retainers around the place, one of them with a character who was to become, albeit briefly, the most talked-about owner in the sport. Terry Ramsden was small-time in those years, still making the money-market fortune he was later so dramatically to lose. His racing obsession began quietly enough, putting a couple of horses with a middle-of-the-road Newmarket trainer named David Dale. Being on the spot, I was engaged to ride them and, although neither was a world-beater, they were good enough to win races around the country tracks. Each time I rode for him, Terry sent his chauffeur round with a present for me. I was shrewd enough to encourage the potential of this arrangement by telling him that his filly needed a lot of racing, but I was not canny enough to foresee the impact he would have on the sport in later years, the years when money was no object and when he patronised big yards, such as Jenny Pitman's and Mick Easterby's, with horses purchased specifically to win major prizes.

Even if I could have known what was coming, we were destined to fall out. Terry was a flamboyant man who loved to surround himself with acolytes and, even at this stage, he had appointed a racing manager who, naturally enough, tried to justify his salary by aiming high. Terry's third horse was a juvenile hurdler named General Concorde. He had cost a bit more than the other two and Terry now clearly craved the flavour of the big time. He started him off sensibly enough, though, running him on a Monday at Plumpton. He finished second, running too free early on but finishing well to be beaten by only a length-and-a-half. I was pleased with him and thought he would certainly win another race of similar quality. Terry and his racing manager had loftier ideas. They wanted to send him to Haydock for the Victor Ludorum Hurdle, and then on to Cheltenham for the Triumph.

There were a number of factors, I thought, conspiring against this plan. One was lack of time. The Haydock race was five days off, Cheltenham a mere twelve days after that. Committing a previously unraced hurdler to that sort of programme was fanciful, at best. My overriding concern, though, was that General Concorde simply would not be good enough. It is never easy to tell a bullish owner, or trainer for that matter, that he should aim a little lower with his pride and joy, but I did my best with Terry, imploring him to miss Haydock, partly because it would come too soon but primarily because I knew for a fact there was at least one horse in the field he could not beat. Nick Henderson was running Childown, who had won three times under Hywel Davies since joining the yard and was running at Haydock as a final preliminary for the Cheltenham race, for which he was ante-post favourite. Nick had booked me to ride him for the first time and, much as I enjoyed the fruits of my link with Terry Ramsden, I was not about to pass up such a top ride to partner a newcomer who had just finished second at Plumpton.

Terry took no notice. Egged on, I suspect, by his paid advisor, he insisted on going to Haydock and, against all logic, backing General Concorde to beat Childown and a host of other decent young hurdlers. He booked David Dutton to ride the horse and he trailed in ninth of eleven. I won the race by a fast-diminishing head, but I never rode for Terry again. Furthermore, I lost the ride on Childown to John Francome at Cheltenham, where he was eventually displaced as favourite by a late rush of money for a newcomer to the Henderson yard called See You Then. The future champion finished second. Childown? He cleared only two flights before breaking his leg and having to be put down. So this confused and unsatisfactory saga had no happy endings.

It was nothing new to me to ride for owners who might be headstrong, eccentric or possibly both. I have seen any number who apparently identified racing as a good and glamorous way to spend some of the money they have made in a booming business. They can be a godsend to a trainer, because they often come into the game with the gung-ho attitude that they have made all this money and, come what may, they are going to enjoy it. So they can be led, like lambs to the slaughter, into paying often unrealistic prices for jumping horses. Then, their egos suitably pampered and their dreams nourished by persistent talk of champion breeding, they start thinking about private boxes at Cheltenham, swanking to their business partners about their Gold Cup hope ... and so it goes on until, in all but a few

fortunate cases, the bubble bursts. Either the money runs out or
the horses turn out to be not quite the stuff of dreams. Much
the poorer, and severely disillusioned, these transitory owners
then slip away to make a bit more spending money, which they
will then direct into some other pursuit.

Ramsden never made it that far. He had been good for racing,
putting a lot of money into sponsorship and a lot more, admirably
discreetly, towards worthy causes. His style and his image had
also created interest, which is never a bad thing, and while the
horses were winning and business was thriving, it looked for a
time as if he might, after all, be a survivor. But, like many others
in his line of work, the stock market crash wiped him out, and
he was a sad fugitive from business, racing and from his own
country, when last he made headlines in the press.

A more familiar route was taken by a man called David Steele,
who burst onto the scene in 1984 through the exploits of two
young hurdlers trained by John Jenkins.

In a single season, Beat the Retreat won nine races for Mr
Steele and Wing and a Prayer won five. The link with the previous
tale is ironical – at Sandown Park in December of that year. I
won the Mecca three-year-old hurdle on Beat the Retreat, beating
a much more fancied animal by a head. The runner-up was Wing
and a Prayer, trained at the time by Alan Bailey and owned, you
guessed it, by Terry Ramsden. Before the weekend was out, Mr
Steele and Mr Ramsden had talked terms and the horse had
changed owners and stables. John Francome subsequently won
four times on him, and I won once, before he finished down the
field at both Cheltenham and Liverpool.

Beat the Retreat was my sort of ride. Of his fourteen races
that season, I rode him in only four, but we won three of those
and, in each case, I was never headed. 'Made all, hard ridden,
ran on well,' is the usual summary of his performances, just the
way I like to ride a tough young hurdler. This, though, was an
example of building up from the bottom. Beat the Retreat's first
three outings were at Fontwell, Bangor and Plumpton. He won
them all but then, upped in class to run at Cheltenham, Kempton
and Sandown, he was beaten each time and had to go back to
rustic old Plumpton to get back in the winner's enclosure.

By mid-November he had already run seven times but John
Jenkins was not about to go easy on him. He ran another seven

times in the ensuing ten weeks, producing five wins, a second and one fall. He was quick, genuine and a pleasure to ride. He probably also gave his owner the wrong idea about the racing game.

David Steele came over as a very nice guy with no real grasp of reality. Because he had struck lucky, largely through the training talent of John Jenkins, in his first serious year as an owner, he expected every other year to take the same happy course. It just doesn't work that way in racing. For the following season, he spent £100,000 on an Irish-bred horse called Ivy League. He turned out to be next-to-useless and I think the experience soured David, utterly disillusioning him with a sport which had been so unusually kind to him.

The last I heard, he had diverted his enthusiasm into motor racing and was driving his own car on the saloon racing circuit. In this, it seems, he was every bit as fanatical as he had been as a racehorse owner. He stayed with John Jenkins one night, en route to some event at Snetterton, and when John was making tea at dawn the following day, he was startled to see David descend the stairs in full driver's regalia, silk scarf and all. He was not due to race until late afternoon but, as he had in the horse game, he was intent on living every second of the part.

Another eccentric owner in the Jenkins stable was Freddie Starr, the comedian. The first ride I had for him was in a novice hurdle at Fakenham, prior to which we had never met. But, as I emerged from the weighing-room and headed for the parade ring, I knew Freddie by his familiar face and he knew me because I was wearing his colours. I do not embarrass easily but what happened next came very close to achieving it. Freddie had been standing on the farthest edge of the ring but, on seeing me, he set off across the grass at a sprint, scattering stewards and dowager ladies before finally taking a flying leap into my arms. Almost knocking me over, he then showered me with kisses, to the plain astonishment of everyone around.

Despite first impressions, Freddie was not just into racing as a self-promotion exercise. Extrovert he most certainly is, but he genuinely likes the game and he had one or two useful horses. I rode him a few winners until our relationship, like so many others in this fickle business, came to an end through an unexpected, and in this case unjust defeat.

Early in the 1985–86 season, I won on a handicap chaser called Kings Bridge. Owner Starr, trainer Jenkins. His win, at Newbury, had been a slight surprise but, having discovered that he was useful, a race was mapped out for him at Devon a week later. Freddie travelled down and was at his most exuberant in the parade ring, defeat apparently not even a consideration. I too thought the horse would win but I came up against a worthy rival in one ridden by Brendan Powell and we duelled, neck and neck, over the last three fences.

When my horse began to go sharply left-handed after the last, I sensed he had broken down but, in situations such as that, you have to try and win. I used the whip to keep him straight but he ran away from it, drifting across the other horse and, quite patently, causing some accidental interference. By then, however, Brendan's horse was dog tired and mine, whatever his leg problem, was galloping on resolutely. We won by seven lengths and although, after jumping off to lead my horse back, I heard there was to be a stewards' inquiry, I could not believe they would take the race away from such an emphatic winner.

That they did so was sickening enough for us all, but Freddie did not take the decision at all well. He lodged an appeal, which had to be heard by the stewards of the Jockey Club at Portman Square, and then instructed me to attend on his behalf. I had every good intention of being there, too, but on the appointed day I encountered every conceivable hazard, from snow through accidents to traffic jams, on the road to London, and eventually had to telephone to say I would not make it. I had two booked rides for Nick Henderson at Warwick and, as I felt my evidence would have next to no bearing on the inquiry, I turned around to make sure of at least meeting one engagement on the day. I rode a winner for Nick but that did nothing to appease Freddie, who plainly blamed me for the failure of his appeal. He has not spoken to me from that day to this.

I have never quite known where I stand with John Jenkins because, shrewd trainer though he is, his jockey arrangements have never been the most organised. Kings Bridge provided a case in point. The night before he won at Newbury, I phoned John to ask him about a hurdler he was planning to run that weekend. He did not mention Kings Bridge and, so far as I was concerned, he had obviously booked someone else for the ride.

But he hadn't. Next morning, the day of the race, he was back on the phone at breakfast time asking me to ride him. As he was due to carry the minimum ten stone, I could have done with a little more notice.

This, however, was not unusual for John. Having come from the regimented background of Tom Jones's yard, I have always been in the habit of telephoning all my regular trainers on a Sunday in order to pencil in probable rides for the week ahead. Trainers' plans will inevitably vary according to weather, opposition and horses' health but it is normally possible to create a skeleton list of riders. Not with John. Week after week, he was unable to tell me for sure what he might want me to ride on the Monday, let alone the rest of the week.

I remember scanning the *Sporting Life* one morning and seeing that John had a runner, forecast to be favourite, with no named jockey. I phoned him immediately and, to my amazement, he said he had not booked anyone. I promptly booked myself and the horse duly won. On another occasion, I rang him about some runners a few days ahead and he casually asked what I was doing later that day. On being told I had a day off, he asked if I could get down to Fontwell to ride a novice hurdler for him. That too, was a winner.

His late changes of plan, and generally laid-back approach to riding arrangements, have led to some unpleasantness at times and I once had to act as mediator between John and Philip Mitchell when they threatened to come to blows outside the Plumpton weighing-room over which of them had booked Simon Sherwood for their horse in a juvenile hurdle. I felt slightly miffed when I offered by services to them both and neither seemed keen to take me up!

For all this, for all the frustrations of riding for John, the knowledge that his is a gambling stable and the impression that he has sometimes been surrounded by some insalubrious characters, the Jenkins yard continues to turn out winners both on the flat and over jumps. Like Martin Pipe, John works closely with his very astute father, and his horses are always turned out looking magnificently fit.

It was this ability to get his string fitter than other people's which enabled John to clean up at the early jumps meetings during the mid-eighties. One year, he turned out sixteen winners in the first eight days, all of them ridden by John Francome. With that sort of launch pad, John was clear of the field, and well on his way to another jockeys' championship, before some of us were properly aware that the season has started.

Not for the only time in my career, I was basically living off Francome's scraps but it was a far from mean diet. There were enough horses to keep us both pretty busy and one, in particular, stands out. I am not sure how many races Kyoto ended up winning but it must have been twenty-odd, and I reckon I rode half that number. At his peak, he would win six or seven in a season, always on fast ground and around the sharp country tracks like Newton Abbot or Fakenham. He was not outstanding but John placed him brilliantly, and he was still winning, in suitable company, at the age of twelve.

Kyoto gave me plenty of good days but also one memorably bad one, when he set off the odds-on favourite for a three-runner chase at Uttoxeter and the left-hand rein snapped as we landed over the first fence. Kyoto was a hard puller and so this was no laughing matter. I still had a serviceable right rein but, by pulling on that, I only made him veer right-handed which, as Uttoxeter is a left-handed track, was distinctly unhelpful. The water jump was upon us before I could implement any plan and he popped that safely enough. Then, grabbing a handful of mane with my left hand, I tried my best to slow him down. It was hopeless. The third fence loomed up and, seeing a stride, I gave him a kick and we went for it. He was a good jumper and we landed in front and intact, but the shape of the course was such that I had no earthly hope of navigating him round. In desperation, and with the rare but real feeling of fear growing in me, I reached right under his neck and grabbed him by the bit-rings, simply as a means of telling him something was wrong. Thank God, it seemed to get through to him and, as he slowed to a steady canter, I was able to jump off.

All this had seemed quite a vivid drama to me but most of the punters were evidently oblivious of the spectacle. As I led Kyoto back, the broken rein trailing from my free hand, I was subjected to a stream of foulmouthed abuse from those who had done their money and had not bothered to see why. At times like that, I despair of the betting public.

Chapter Nine

'To overcome persistent leg problems and win three Champion Hurdles is enough in some people's eyes to merit See You Then being declared the greatest of them all. But because See You Then ran so infrequently, his detractors will inevitably harp on that fact as some kind of deficiency or failing on his part ... In Henderson's words, "He was always a mystery horse". But he was a character and a half all the same, possibly the nastiest piece of work to win the Champion Hurdle since Clair Soleil.'

Michael Tanner, *The Champion Hurdle*

Just as a singer will invariably be associated with one special song, or an actor with one long-running series, so the name of a particular horse is often inseparable from his jockey's. We may not always approve, we may sometimes wish to be remembered for other deeds, but like the singer and his catchiest song, we have no choice. The public decides how we will be remembered and, when my riding career is finally put to rest, there is not the slightest doubt which horse will feature in the epitaph.

Go back ten years or so and Tingle Creek would still have tripped off the tongues of most racegoers when my name was mentioned. To those with long memories, maybe he still does; he was that kind of horse. But while my personal affection for him, and the debt I owe him, remain undiminished, history has dictated that the most joyful jumper I ever rode, the apple of everyone's eye, must make way for a bad-legged, bad-tempered

100

creature whose foreign owners gave every impression of not caring a damn about the horse or the sport. See You Then was a trial to Nick Henderson and me in many ways but he was an undoubtedly great champion and I doubt if I shall ever ride another as good.

My relationship with See You Then stretched over six seasons but involved only eleven races. It began in high drama and ended in unnecessary anti-climax when, against all odds, he was nursed back from apparently terminal injuries to run again at the age of ten. It was the only mistake Nick ever made with the horse, and his four runs that season, three unplaced and one fall, took just a little of the shine from what should have been an untarnished memory.

Other horses have won the Champion Hurdle three times and their names are legendary in the sport – Persian War, Sir Ken and Hatton's Grace. I have no idea how See You Then would have fared in any fantasy match with this trio; all I do know with certainty is that if any of the three had to overcome the perennial problems our horse encountered, then everyone connected was a hero. I don't think I ever fully appreciated Nick's qualities as a trainer until this horse came along. To bring him back for a second and then a third Champion was one of the greatest training feats I have witnessed, and I remain convinced he would have become the first horse to win four but for a fateful February day at Wincanton just before the 1988 Festival.

The See You Then saga was essentially a team success, Nicky very much the captain but others in his yard playing a full part. No one was more important than Glyn Foster. Glyn was the stable-lad in charge of the horse and, in his day, he enjoyed as much media exposure as Janice Coyle was later to have through Desert Orchid. Glyn deserved every bit of it. He also deserved a medal for gallantry every time he went in See You Then's box, because this was a horse with a kink. He had been gelded as a yearling but it made no difference to his temperament. He was a savage.

On his first day in Nick's yard, he pinned Glyn in the corner of his box and tried to kick him while, simultaneously, twisting his head to bite him. Somehow, through daily contact, bullying and cajoling, Glyn earned a truce from the horse, but no one else was allowed near him. He had taken an instant dislike to Nick and continued to show a violent disrespect all the time he was in training there. As for me, I was more than happy to stay well away from his box and to save my meetings with him for the days when it mattered.

But ours, as I say, was a marriage made in drama and coincidence, for we might never have linked up at all but for an untrustworthy horse in the neighbouring stable of Fred Winter. His name was The Reject and John Francome was never in love with him even before the momentous events of 12 March 1985. The Reject had plenty of pace and ability but he was prone to making disastrous mistakes. He was later to convince John to announce his retirement when falling at Chepstow in April but, at Cheltenham, he was no better than an outsider for the Arkle Chase, the two-mile novices championship, and he duly got no further than the second fence.

Falling at the Festival is galling enough. What followed was much, much worse. Somehow, John's left foot was caught in the iron and, as the horse picked himself up, dazed and disorientated, John found himself hanging upside down. If The Reject had run off or, still more alarming, tried to jump another fence, the best we could have hoped for was Franc coming out of it alive. Thankfully, he stayed still enough for one of the groundsmen to come to John's aid, holding the horse's head while the foot was disentangled from the iron.

I was oblivious to all this at the time. My attention was still on the race, trying to persuade Nick's Destiny Bay into contention. It proved a hopeless task and we finished tailed off behind a high-class first three of Boreen Prince, Buck House and Very Promising. This was our second disappointment of the day, because in the opening event, the Supreme Novices Hurdle, Maganyos was similarly detached. She had won a decent conditions race at Chepstow only three days earlier and it had always seemed an ambitious plan to send her straight on to Cheltenham. But Nick had travelled in hope and now, transparently as ever, he was dismayed by his first two runners and none too pleased, it seemed, with their jockey.

I trudged back to weigh in feeling a touch disconsolate. Although I was back riding a lot of Nick's horses on a freelance basis, I had to ride in the Champion Hurdle. See You Then had been John's ride all season. He had run four times leading up to

Cheltenham, winning twice, and the closest look I had had at him was when I rode Jeff King's Joy Ride at Ascot and got beaten by only two lengths. I did not think, on that form, he was good enough to win a Champion Hurdle and neither, it seemed, did J. Francome. When he came back into the weighing-room, not visibly any the worse for his mishap, he blandly told me that he was giving up the ride.

Still unaware of the harrowing escape he had just endured, I didn't believe him at first. Just another Francome prank, I thought, and began changing into the colours of Bajan Sunshine for my promising ride in the Stayers' Hurdle. But it soon dawned that he was serious. He later told me he had not known whether to laugh or cry when he had been released from his undignified hanging agony, but that it had been one of the few times in his career when terror had been his prime emotion. He just didn't feel up to riding See You Then. I also suspect he didn't fancy him, though.

Nick came in and confirmed that I was to take over. I had precisely ten minutes to get ready for the Champion Hurdle. Probably the best way, as things turned out. No time to worry, no time to overcomplicate, just get into the colours, out to the parade ring and on the horse's back.

See You Then was sent off at 16–1. An absolute snip, in hindsight, but on form there was nothing to suggest he could beat Monica Dickinson's horse Browne's Gazette, who had rattled off four highly impressive wins, including the Christmas Hurdle at Kempton. See You Then had finished third there, twenty-five lengths adrift. Students of the formbook justifiably took the view that there was no way he could make up twenty-five lengths on the same terms, so Browne's Gazette was made the odds-on favourite.

There had been no chance for me to evaluate all this in the few minutes before the race but, as it was obvious that Browne's Gazette was a very decent horse, I was only too happy to see him falter at the start. He swerved violently left as the tapes went up and gave away twenty lengths or so, too much even for an odds-on shot to make up in a championship race run on fast ground and at a cracking good pace.

Nicky had told me that See You Then was best held up for a late run, so I tucked him in behind the leaders, feeling pleasantly gratified at how well we were travelling. Coming down the hill and jumping the second last, I stole a look around and could hardly believe my eyes. Mine appeared to be the only runner still on the bridle. Never having ridden the horse, I could only guess at what he held in reserve but I now had only one ahead of me, the former champion Gaye Brief, and Richard Linley was so hard at work on him that I knew I could take him when I chose.

I waited until we had jumped the last, a length adrift, then pressed the accelerator and felt the indescribable thrill of power to the touch. In a matter of strides, we were clear and I knew instinctively it was over. There was no need for the whip, just a spot of nudging to keep him up to his work as he came home, top gear not needed, one of the easiest seven-length winners I ever sat on.

There was a sense of unreality about it all, as if I had blundered into someone else's dream. I recall walking the horse back past the seethingly packed stands with an uncontrollable grin on my face, wondering first if this had really happened and then what on earth I would say to Franc. As ever after a big race, though, the odd circumstances are irrelevant. If John felt any resentment, which I very much doubt, he ably disguised it in the general melee of back-slapping congratulations. It put me on a high that I had probably not experienced from any winner for some years, and after I had won the day's final race, on Alan Jarvis's Kathies Lad, I fancy I might have celebrated with a glass or two of scotch.

The ride had come to me in such a late and unexpected fashion that I could, at the time, feel no special involvement with the horse. I was pleased for Nick, who wore his heart on his sleeve in his usual endearing way, but it was only later, when Franc retired, the ride became unarguably mine and plans for the future were discussed, that I learned a little of See You Then's past.

He was bred to be a classic flat horse, with a sire and dam who were both trained in their day by Sir Noel Murless. He actually won four flat races in Ireland when trained by Con Collins but it was after his final win there, over hurdles, that he came to Lambourn. He was bought by the Marquis Cugliemi di Vulci, the Italian owner of the Stype Wood Stud, with the primary intention of winning the Triumph Hurdle before going to race in Italy. Through no fault of Nick Henderson, who only took charge of him just before the 1984 Festival, that plan failed on both counts. Backed down to an absurdly short 5–2 favourite for the toughest betting race of the year, See You Then was only second to Northern Game, ironically trained in Ireland in the Triumph. He did win a race in Italy but then, apparently, injured himself in a fall on the roads and Nick, who had not expected to see or hear of him again, was alerted to the fact that he was back in England on the owner's stud. Contact was made, plans were revised and the rest, as they say, is history.

It is really not my business to criticise the approach of any owner. After all, they pay the bills which keep the wheels of our game turning, and I suppose they are entitled to be obsessive, indifferent or anything in between. But these Italians got under my skin because they seldom even matched up to a description of indifferent.

The Marquis never came over to watch See You Then run in all the years I rode him. Not even a third Champion Hurdle, and a share of history, could lure him. His daughter came a couple of times before she was the victim of a kidnap back in her home country. I had no contact with the Marquis, and no congratulations from him, until he invited me over to have dinner with him after the third Cheltenham win. As for Nicky, I know his dealings with the Italians largely revolved around an annual battle to dissuade them from taking the horse back over there to race.

What depressed me more than anything was that the owners simply did not seem interested. I have ridden for so many good, loyal owners who, year after year, have suffered horses with limited ability and no luck. These people would give their right arm for a horse half as good as See You Then, and yet he was owned by a miserable man who had no appreciation of the enviable possession in his grasp and no enthusiasm for the involvement which makes the jumping game what it is.

In 1985, however, such gripes were far from my mind. Looking around the crop of leading hurdlers, I began to realise that my first Champion Hurdle ought not to be my last. See You Then stood head and shoulders above his contemporaries and, although it was probably fair to say that the 1985 Champion had not been a vintage one, I saw no reason to suppose that 1986 would be markedly superior.

But I had also learned that the horse was fragile. He did not look it, this big, rounded dark beast, nor did he behave like it when trying to take lumps out of trainer, vet or anyone else unfortunate enough to come within biting distance. But his legs were like china. He had got through five races well enough in the 1984–85 season but he never managed that many again and Nick knew it would be folly to try. He had summered well, pampered in the way a champion is entitled to be, and when he came back into the Windsor House yard, Nick knew there was no way he would be fit for a race before Christmas, or even at the big festive meeting at Kempton. We waited patiently, the press and public slightly less patiently, until mid-January. Even then, he did not reappear competitively, but in a specially arranged racecourse gallop against a couple of stablemates.

It was staged at the end of a Saturday afternoon card at Kempton Park and, such was the interest in the horse, most of the crowd stayed behind to watch. The press had, predictably, begun to have fun with headlines like 'See You When', but their scepticism disappeared when they saw him make mincemeat of his two galloping opponents. He jumped as quickly and precisely as ever and I was happy to tell the assembled hacks that I considered he had come on ten pounds since the previous season. I might have added, though discretion narrowly stopped me, that I could see no way he would be beaten at Cheltenham. To be honest, that piece of public work was as much of a relief to me as it evidently was to the trainer. More had been expected of me that season than at any other stage in my career. With Franc retiring, I had achieved that first-day ambition by graduating to the number-one peg in the weighing-room, the senior jockey. But I had also taken a new retainer with Nicky Henderson, who seemed to have his most powerful string to date, and there was plenty of speculation that the odd couple – the rebellious city gent and the double-barrelled miner's son – could between them clean up both the trainers' and jockeys' titles. Probably for the first time, I also felt I had a genuine chance and, as the first half of the season ended, I was tucked in behind Simon Sherwood in second place. Nick still had a lot of cards to play and I was quietly hopeful of giving it a real go.

January was a depressant. It was one of those months when everything went wrong. Good things were beaten, too many of my rides fell, giving me some unpleasant aches and pains, and the weather turned fickle, so that meetings were abandoned for everything from frost to fog and waterlogging.

Most worrying of all was that my relationship with Nicky was already cracking at the seams, so soon after a resumption of contract terms. He was demanding, and in his position he had a perfect right to be, but I often found I was turning down good outside rides while Nicky agonised over which horses he might run, and where. By the time he made up his mind, it was often too late to recover the spares, and when that happens, a trainer is not guaranteed to come back. It was a good job, one which most jockeys would have been delighted to have. But two things began to impress themselves on me – first, the confirmation of my suspicion that I remained a free spirit at heart, and secondly, that Nicky and I were never likely to enjoy a smooth working relationship. We were just too different.

There was no doubt that See You Then was getting to him in a big way. Every trainer wants to have a champion but, once you have one, the responsibility is great, and if you are a naturally fretful person like Nicky, the pressure must be intense. We jockeys only bear the burden on the relatively few times we actually sit on the horse's back; for the trainer, the potential for worry is present twenty-four hours a day, seven days a week. With a bad-legged horse, owned from afar by people with unusual priorities, it is easy to see why Nick sometimes gave the impression he had not slept for a week.

His state of mind had not been helped on the early January morning when we schooled See You Then for the first time since his summer break. I think the horse was intent on showing us just how fresh and well he was. His method was to buck me off, violently and irresistibly, just as soon as I swung my leg across him.

The mental image was frightening. Here I was, ten weeks away from defending the championship on the best hurdler I was ever likely to ride, and he was about to charge unchecked across the Berkshire downs, his suspect legs prone to heaven knows what fate. As I hit the ground with a resounding thud, I caught a fleeting glimpse of Nick's distraught face, and knew he was suffering the same unthinkable dread.

As much by luck as judgement, I had managed to hang onto

the reins in one hand and See You Then, contenting himself with a haughty look of superior pleasure, did not even try to increase my indignities by dragging me along the deck. I picked myself up to a chorus of well-chosen oaths from the trainer, uttered more in relief than rage, and carefully reunited myself with the horse. I needn't have worried. He had proved his point, displayed his strength and masculinity, and was now perfectly happy to show off his matchless hurdling talent on the schooling grounds.

January came to a painful end, and an alarming one. Three days before See You Then's long-intended comeback race, the Oteley Hurdle at Sandown, I stupidly took a ride for Roddy Armytage on a novice chaser I had never sat on before. Roddy had a good record with his young chasers, which might have persuaded me, but it was still a senseless risk, for which I paid dearly. The horse, Two Eagles, was brought down in his race at Windsor and I was galloped over by one landing behind us. The casualties were my nose, more an aesthetic and ego problem than one which might stop me riding, and my wrist, which for several minutes I feared was broken.

I felt obliged to give up my last ride of the day and, in keeping with the way things were going, Peter Scudamore took the mount and won. It was a hurdler of Nick's which even he believed had no chance but Scu had begun to ride with the pumped-up confidence which was to carry him to his first outright jockeys' title.

I had to suffer a couple of uncomfortable days, and several anxious telephone calls from N. Henderson, before proving my fitness by riding a novice chaser for him at Sandown on the Friday. Somewhat to my surprise, I won on him and reported back to Esher the following lunchtime with the adrenalin flowing freely for my reunion with the champ.

Most jockeys' favourite courses are to some extent dictated by memories, and the spine-tingling rides I had on Tingle Creek would have been enough to make Sandown seem special to me. But there is more. For spectators, Sandown is a natural theatre of a course, with some of the best viewing facilities in the country and, invariably, some of the best racing to view. For jockeys and trainers, it is a joy, run with efficiency and flair, virtues which seldom go together in our sport. Season after season, Sandown produces memorable jump racing and, on that first day of

February 1986, it excelled itself with a shared top bill of Burrough Hill Lad in the feature chase and See You Then in the hurdle.

Both horses won impressively, and in the case of my horse the great thing was that he effortlessly gave away weight to some decent handicappers while still burly and unfit.

Burrough Hill Lad, who had won the Cheltenham Gold Cup two years previously, was ridden for the first time by Peter Scudamore. It was not a universally popular switch because it involved the jocking-off, sacking if you like, of the popular northern-based rider Phil Tuck, who had won the Gold Cup and any number of other races on the horse. But it was not Scu's job to take a moral line; like the rest of us, he is a professional, seeking to ride the best horses he can. The fact that he was chosen for the ride exemplified his burgeoning stature at that time. Not only was he soon to begin a lengthy reign as champion jockey, he was also achieving a celebrity status which his with-drawn personality had never actively sought.

He has learned to handle it well in subsequent years. Back in those days, he liked to let his riding talk for him and, quite simply, to ride as many horses as he could. His hunger for winners took him anywhere and everywhere and, I have to admit, formed quite a contrast with my own outlook. I had become increasingly choosy about outside rides and increasingly inclined to stay at home if the rides on offer on a particular day amounted to a couple of unknown novices. Peter would go and ride them and, because he gave it everything, was unfailingly willing and polite and, in the way that these things run, had the force of fortune with him, he was riding winners on no-hopers and, inevitably, picking up enviable spares. It had become clear to me now that Scu was a far more likely champion than me; it is clear to me now that he probably wanted it more and so deserved it more, too.

I can be critical of myself at this distance of time and I am aware that I had begun to coast through life, expecting the winners to come to me rather than going out to graft for them as I had done in the early days. I could be an awkward bugger to deal with in a working situation, and I am sure my cocksure complacency was a contributory factor to the problems that Nicky and I continued to experience. His unquestioning, uncomplaining dedication to his job could make him an insular character when compared with me but in the weeks left to us between the Sandown run and the Champion Hurdle, our concern over the horse manifested itself in very different ways. Nick stayed up all night in the arctic temperatures of Lambourn, while I went skiing in France!

A week into February, the frosts began in earnest. Not just the sort which leave a festive sprinkling of white, first thing, and vanish from the ground as soon as the sun appears, but the frost which digs deep, clamping its grip on the country for days or even weeks at a time. Racing, at least on turf, is one of the first casualties of such a freeze-up and, as the weather forecasters grimly assured us that we were in for a long one, I organised a trip to the piste.

I remember having a passing flash of conscience, a feeling that I was almost daring the fates to do their worst with me as I hurtled down a ski-slope in my unpolished fashion a mere month before the biggest meeting of the year. But then I just set about enjoying myself and, as usual, succeeded.

I came home a week later to find the English weather much as it had been on the ski-slopes, no promise of a thaw. It was only when I made a cheery phone call to Nicky, just checking myself back in, that the extent of his problems made an impression on me. Exhaustion and panic were jostling for position in his mind, I think, and it was only through his nature that panic was winning. All prospect of getting another run into See You Then before the big day had been banished by the weather, which would not have been so serious but for the inevitable fact that the Lambourn gallops were unusable. All that was left was Nick's all-weather paddock and even that had proved to be not quite all-weather. The ferocity and regularity of the frost was such that the strip would have been rock-hard, utterly useless, but for the nightly use of the Henderson tractor, harrowing it at two-hourly intervals. In such bitter cold, it was not an appealing job but Nicky has never been one to duck out through delegation and he was doing most of the tractor driving himself. It was devotion beyond the call of duty, and I doubt if he ever received any thanks for it from the Italian end of the operation, but I believe Nick's nocturnal heroics may well have made the difference between winning and losing the Champion Hurdle that year.

The thaw set in seven days before the start of the Festival –

too close for comfort. It left a lot of horses short of work, a lot of trainers short of sleep and a lot of jockeys short of the fitness which only race-riding can provide. Just as a footballer who has missed several weeks will need a game to get match-fit, so it is with us. I had been running, much against my inner will, and had even worked out on a rowing machine. I had cut down on food and drink too, but I knew that it would take a ride or two to put me straight and I was glad to get them in over the weekend. Then, following my suspicious custom, I took the Monday off and drove over to stay in Cheltenham that night, slightly more quietly than the thousands of Irishmen who had begun the traditional invasion.

Cheltenham is the highlight of my year and never, before or since, has it lived up to expectations quite as it did in 1986. To win the big hurdle again was my main objective and simply achieving that aim would have satisfied me. But the week was full of heady memories, and they began in the very first race of the meeting.

My ride in the Supreme Novices Hurdle was River Ceiriog and he was an unusual runner in the race through still being a maiden. He had run decently in his previous outing at Ascot but, to my mind, his starting price of 40–1 was an accurate reflection of his chance in such a hot event. Imagine my amazement, then, when I hit the front on him at the top of the hill, stole a look over my shoulder after jumping the second last and had a rapid double-take to confirm my impression that nothing else was going remotely as well. My horse strode on up the hill to win, unchallenged, by fifteen lengths, quite the most unexpected Cheltenham winner I have ever enjoyed.

Nick was speechless. At least it might have taken his mind off See You Then for a time, though, knowing him, not for long. But the Champion went equally well for us. I thought See You Then still looked to be carrying plenty of condition and fleetingly fretted that Nick might have been unable to get enough work into him. The fear was groundless. In what was virtually a carbon copy of the 1985 race, I cruised upsides Gaye Brief at the last and we sprinted away to win, once again, by seven lengths.

He was so far ahead of his rivals in terms of class that his delayed and interrupted preparation cost us nothing. Nick's selfless efforts had paid off and if the biggest field for more than twenty years had gathered in anticipation of a vulnerable crown, they had sadly underestimated our horse.

The rest of the festival might have been an anti-climax, but I had a couple of exciting rides in defeat and took a full part in one of the greatest, and certainly the most emotional Gold Cup of my career. My ride was Run and Skip, who might be damned with faint praise by being called a mere handicapper. He was, however, at the top of his form that year and had won several races through stirring, resolute front-running. I intended to use the same tactics again, fully aware that I would be risking the wrath of all Ireland by taking on the great Dawn Run at the head of affairs.

We were still in front three from home and we finished fourth. I was proud to end up so close behind a three-horse battle which must now be replayed more often on TV than any other jump-racing clip, and to be witness to the unique scenes which followed Jonjo's win on Dawn Run. But my enduring memory of that race is the noise. Cheltenham in March is the only time I can ever recall being aware of the roar of a crowd and I swear that the deafening din rolling across us from the stands as we neared the post in that marvellous race could have been heard several counties away.

But if mine was a bit part in the Dawn Run show, it was an ongoing star role in the See You Then saga. He suffered an increasingly rare setback when Nick took him to Aintree on Grand National day three weeks later, when he did not seem to like the course, the sticky ground or the two-mile five-furlong trip. Nick also concluded that it had been a mistake to even contemplate going back to the well again after Cheltenham and so, for the following season, we settled on a programme of one prep race, Cheltenham and finish. It was not a programme designed to show off the horse to his fans, which explains why See You Then never did attain the popularity of certain lesser lights who ran much more often, but it was undoubtedly the right programme for him.

Nick was seldom without his problems even within such an unambitious schedule, however, and now it was an inflamed corn which plagued horse and trainer. See You Then was confined to the yard for weeks on end, just at the time he should have been doing some serious work. Nick kept him on the go in his equine swimming pool, an absolute godsend, but it still seemed that we might have to take a massive risk and go to Cheltenham without a prior run.

I think it was Corky Browne, Nicky's wise old head lad, whose voice was the persuasive one now. There was a conditions race at Haydock eleven days before the Champion and Corky thought the horse should go for it. Nick was dubious, and so was I – he patently wasn't fit – but Corky won the day, we went to Haydock and won a three-horse race in soft ground without undue concern. A racecourse gallop at Sandown was a further help but we still arrived at Prestbury Park on 17 March with cause for apprehension. The race bore it out.

There were eighteen runners this time, five fewer than the previous year, and my horse went off at 11–10 against rather than the 6–5 on in 1986. There were those, obviously, who shared our concerns. In the parade ring, the rituals were faithfully followed. Nick gave me instructions, repeating himself for the sake of something to say to smother his nerves. We both knew that I would ride him the same way I always did, keeping hold of him until the last flight and steering a course through the middle to outer of the pack.

My raceriding instinct is habitually to go around the inside, the shortest way, but on this horse I never took the risk. I once lost the County Hurdle at the Festival by sticking to the inner and finding myself hopelessly blocked when I tried to make my run. In big fields and on that course, it is asking for trouble; at the fourth last, the rail forces the horses to concertina at the very point of the race when the no-hopers, having had their moment of glory up front, are beginning to drop back through the field. If you are on the inside, there is no way through, and each time I rode See You Then, I would hear anguished cries at that stage from jockeys trapped on the rail. I just smiled to myself and kicked on.

Despite this being the premier hurdle of the season, the championship race, there has regularly been a horse or two in the field which had no logical right to be running at that level. They are always worth looking out for. In 1986, Oliver Carter, a west country permit-holder, ran one which would have been much more in his element at Devon and Exeter, and I found myself tracking him as the race began in earnest. We were nearing a hurdle and I suddenly knew I did not want to be following this horse across it. I pulled to the far outside and, sure enough, he fell. If I had followed my original course I would almost certainly have been brought down.

There were no traffic problems in 1987. Nothing at all. I woke up the horse at the top of the hill and felt the familiar surge of power under me, as close to a feeling of invincibility as I have ever known. He flew the second last and was going almost too well. Not wanting to hit the front yet, I eased back on the throttle, allowing David Elsworth's Barnbrook Again to go on, then pressed ahead again, jumping to the front at the last and going for home. It was *déjà vu* for the horse and rider until, halfway up the hill, I knew something was different. The petrol tank read empty.

I didn't dare look around. The road from the stands told me that one was coming to challenge and, for the first time in three Champion Hurdles, I had to get serious with See You Then. We held on by a length-and-a-half, comfortable enough in the context of the race if a bit tight in terms of our own limited history, and although the postmortems blamed Jerry Fishback, on the American runner-up Flatterer, for allowing me first run, it is complete hypothesis whether that made any difference or not. The post had come in time, which was all that mattered to me, and my only alarm in three years of riding the champion had lasted no more than a few seconds.

Winning two Champion Hurdles with such a problem horse would have been an outstanding training achievement. To win three was a horse-racing miracle. Four was fantasy land, and so disappointment, rather than surprise, was the chief emotion when See You Then broke down at Wincanton eleven months later.

He had been ante-post favourite all winter to break the record and Nick was, if anything, more confident about his well-being than for a couple of years. When he went to Wincanton, for what was to be his only prep race, he certainly looked well forward. He was, after all, still only eight years old. If any horse could win a fourth Champion Hurdle, I thought, this had to be the one.

The great irony was that it was not one of the dodgy forelegs which let us down. See You Then broke a bone in one of his previously sound hind legs. He also damaged a suspensory ligament. I knew it was bad when I felt him go beneath me. Just how bad was obvious when I jumped off and watched, disconsolate, as he hobbled mournfully around me. Nick was there quickly and he could not control the tears. After what he had been through with the horse, I had every sympathy, and if my own hardened outlook restricted me to feeling sick at heart but saying nothing, it was a day when sentiment got the better of many.

Nobody at Wincanton that day expected See You Then to run again. It would probably have been better if he had not. But after eighteen months of tender, loving care, the impossible dream was revived. Misguided though it now seems, we saw no reason why he would not win another Champion at the age of ten. We had not bargained for the fact that the long break, the injury and the simple fact of advancing years had taken the edge off him. He was not the same horse, and I prefer to think of it that way, remembering him in his pomp as the best jumper of hurdles I ever sat on, as a horse with an unusually high cruising speed and the devastating ability to quicken up in a matter of strides. He skimmed over the hurdles, never breaking stride, and my favourite memory of all is of the times when I came cosily to the last, one horse ahead of me, the others beaten, knowing I could change gear once, maybe even twice if necessary. He was that good.

Opposite, above The team for Limerick, July 1984. Peter Scudamore, Hywel Davies, John Francome, Jonjo O'Neil, yours truly and Robert Earnshaw. *Below* Not only did Far Bridge stand up, he won by a short head.

Above After winning the Ritz Club trophy, Cheltenham 1985.

117

Me and the boss, Nick Henderson.

Below A feeling impossible to put into words. Cheltenham 1986. *Right* 'Relax, the Champion Hurdle's not till 3.30.'

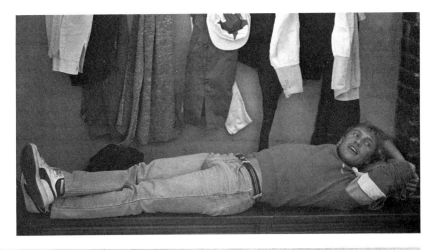

The third consecutive
Champion Hurdle was
so sweet.

'What hit me?'

Chapter Ten

Fools and frauds dominate racing, or so the popular mythology would have us believe. The fiction associated with the sport, both in books and on TV, focuses relentlessly and inevitably on the manipulation of the weak and innocent by the powerfully crooked. Racing comes across as a hotbed of villainy, desperadoes at every turn.

If I say it is not really like that, I am not painting us all as paragons of virtue. Racing folk are not all angels because we work in a gambling industry and, wherever there is gambling, corruption is not far away. Horses do get 'stopped', sometimes at the will of the jockeys but more often under instructions from trainer and/or owner. Horses have also been doped, although the great advances in testing and detection have surely minimised the risk. And there are still times on the racecourse where our tough sport becomes an unscrupulously rough one, although, here again, improved camera patrols mean that very little should escape the eyes of the stewards.

The most damning accusations that can be thrown at a jockey are that he is either corrupt or incompetent. I have been called both in my time, but more often than not the voice has belonged to someone on a racecourse, either staggering out of a bar after too much beer or out of the betting ring with empty pockets. It is amazing how judgement can be jaundiced by backing the wrong horse on a full belly of booze.

A jockey is at his most vulnerable to such slander, when he has been beaten on an odds-on favourite, as I know to my cost from one autumn afternoon at Market Rasen, when my friend and neighbour Gavin Pritchard-Gordon ran a three-year-old called Dhofar, who had won his first hurdle race only five days earlier. It looked a weak field and the bookmakers took no chances, shortening him up to an absurd 5–1 on. Why anyone would want to back a juvenile at odds-on at all, let alone at 5–1 on, I cannot imagine, but someone clearly did, for after Dhofar had been beaten by a northern horse, Tommy Gunner, we were subjected to an unusual and very dangerous attack. I was walking the horse back to unsaddle, wondering which of the possible excuses might actually be relevant, when a big bloke with an ugly expression jumped out in front of us and hurled a handful of coins, accompanied by some unpleasant remark about my honesty. The coins hit Dhofar rather than me, thankfully causing no damage, and the police quickly took the attacker into their care.

The police were busy again on my behalf during a Uttoxeter meeting, one May Bank Holiday. I had gone there with some attractive rides, most of them sure to go off favourite, but the day began badly when the first of them broke down and I had to pull him up in front of the stands. Even to those who cannot recognise the signs of a horse going lame, I would have thought it would be obvious that no jockey who is 'up to something' would be silly enough to pull up in full view of crowd and stewards. Apparently not. I was greeted by some booing and jeering from the ignorant few.

Thinking no more about it, I got on board another favourite in the three-mile chase. He was a lazy horse and I was lying last of the four runners as we entered the straight with more than a circuit still to run, far too early to be worried. Just the other side of the running rail, though, lurked a lunatic intent on revenge for having done this money on me in the previous event. He picked up a dustbin (to this day I don't know what it was doing there) and hurled it at me from close range.

It could have caused mayhem but the idiot had chosen to throw the bin full. Its contents spewed across the course but he was not strong enough to score a hit. The coins incident had alarmed and angered me; this one seemed so ludicrous that I burst out laughing, and passed the winning post with tears of mirth steaming up my goggles. A jockey cannot afford to worry about the occasional punter sounding off. A losing bet is almost always the cause. It is of far greater concern when the complaint comes from the employer, the owner or trainer.

Being a naturally vigorous rider, I think I have probably been accused of 'stopping' a horse less than most. John Francome, whose style was far more tender, found himself accused every other day. It happens to us all sooner or later but the worst, and most hurtful instance in my career involved a race at Kempton Park in November 1988.

I was riding a lot, at the time, for Reg Akehurst, and had enjoyed plenty of success for him with horses such as Inlander, who had won two of the previous year's biggest handicap hurdles, and Juven Light, on whom I had won several times over hurdles. Now, Reg had a new recruit called Man on the Line, a five-year-old who had strengthened up nicely and looked as if he would be a very useful hurdler. First time out, at Chepstow, he was only beaten a head. Three weeks later he was in an eighteen-strong field for a two-and-a-half-mile race at Cheltenham, where to my great satisfaction I got him up in the last stride to beat a fancied horse trained by Nick Henderson, who was by now using Jamie Osborne as his stable jockey. We went on to Kempton, for the Vauxhall Novices Hurdle, and after winning the three-year-old hurdle early in the day for Gavin, I was very confident of completing a double, and did not mind who knew about it.

I probably should have won. I freely admit that. I gave Man on the Line credit for more toe than he possessed; as a result, I could never quite get back at a flat-hardened horse of John Sutcliffe's who had got first run off the final turn. We were beaten four lengths, but the third horse was another twenty-five lengths away. As the winner had recently been placed in the Cesarewitch, defeat was no disgrace, but you would have thought as much from the expression of the owner. Les Randall, of Thrinacia Investment, was far from pleased.

I knew Les well enough and had ridden a few winners for him in the past. Why or how he got it into his head, I still don't know, but he became convinced I had deliberately got his horse beaten. His response was to instruct Reg that I should not ride any of his horses in the future. The ride on Man on the Line passed to Peter Scudamore and he won his next two races – both, significantly, on more galloping tracks than Kempton. For me, it meant more than losing one or two useful rides, because the slur had its effect on Reg Akehurst and he stopped putting me up on all his other horses, too.

The fact that I was innocent was not so important, to me, as being doubted in the first place. I had ridden enough, for both Reg and Les, for them to know me well, and it saddened me that they could have such suspicions. What price loyalty, I thought, but then in racing, as I never cease to discover, loyalty is a rare and precious commodity.

It took four years before, out of the blue, Reg Akehurst phoned up and asked me to ride a novice chaser of his. It won, and if I say so myself, I gave it a hell of a ride. The following week, Reg was on again and to my utter astonishment told me that Les Randall wanted me to ride a couple of horses for him. One of them was a frustrating novice chaser with whom no jockey had been able to strike up a decent relationship. His name? Man on the Line. The story had turned full circle.

In years gone by, or so I am led to believe, the proportion of non-triers was far higher. There were no patrol cameras and so, on remote parts of a course, jockeys would get up to all manner of mischief. It all led to the story, which by now has become an apocryphal part of racing folklore but which I enjoy hearing, attributed to a starter in the north named Colonel Smith. Confronted one day before the introduction of safety limits, by thirty-five runners for a novice hurdle at Catterick, this military gentleman climbed onto his rostrum and barked at the assembled throng, 'Now look here, jockeys. I don't give a damn, but you might as well be safe, so we'll do it this way – triers line up at the front, non-triers at the back.'

Nowadays, although it would be naive to pretend that all horses run on their merits in every race, the huge majority of losers are beaten because they are not good enough. It is this fact which many besotted owners, and the odd blinkered trainer, find it impossible to digest; in their eyes, the jockey must be to blame, ergo he is either crooked or incompetent, maybe both.

The jockey is the easy scapegoat because he is the public partner of the horse. But I have known trainers who could get horses beaten through incompetence, and a few who would get them beaten on purpose. I have also known one who pulled a remarkable stunt after one of his horses had won a race.

The event concerned was a selling handicap chase, almost the last resort in jump racing. It almost goes without saying, then, that the horse I was riding had only limited ability, so I was slightly surprised when the trainer came to me beforehand and said, categorically, that it would win. I was both surprised and bewildered when he added that I should not pull him up immediately we crossed the finishing line, but canter on up to the top corner of the course, before the left turn out of the straight.

Naturally, I asked him why, but he refused to say. 'Just do it,' was all I got out of him. Well, he was right about the race, our horse winning with plenty in hand, and, although I felt slightly foolish, I followed his instructions and let the horse pull up at the top of the course. Suddenly, from the bushes to my right, out jumps the horse's lad clutching a syringe, from which he proceeded to squirt a good quantity of blood up the horse's nostrils.

It all happened so fast that I had no chance to protest or even to query what he was doing, but it did not take long for me to work out the reason. When, eventually, I walked the horse into the winner's enclosure, he had blood trickling from his nose. Not his blood, of course, but the crowd around the enclosure was not to know that. Their conclusion would have been that the horse had broken a blood vessel, which would neatly have explained why he was running below his apparent class in a selling chase. No self-respecting trainer would buy an old handicapper who breaks blood vessels and so, just as the winning trainer had planned, there was no bid at the auction. He retained the horse without paying out and, I am sure, all concerned had a nice touch in the betting ring.

This was an instance of the jockey being an innocent pawn in a game involving owner and trainer, a game which happened to produce a result. All manner of things could have gone wrong, the most likely being that the horse turned out to be not quite the good thing they all expected. I don't know how many good things, on average, go down to the start at every race meeting held in this country. All I do know is that it is a great deal more than the available number of winners.

Jump racing is, by definition, a graveyard for popular dogma. You could stand in a betting shop before any race you like and there will be some clever guy telling anyone who cares to listen that the favourite is 'a stone cold certainty'. He ignores the facts staring him in the face, that there are a minimum of eight and a maximum of thirty-odd obstacles to jump, at any one of which the so-called certainty could fall, slip up, be brought down, carried out or simply decide he did not want to jump it. Then there are minor matters such as traffic problems, fitness, recurrence of old and half-forgotten ailments, suitability of course and going. Or, and I can assure you it happens, the good thing may just be having a bad day, not feeling 100 per cent. It happens to horses as well as humans.

And then there is the jockey to consider. I know there are those who rate the contribution of the man on top pretty low, who believe that if a horse is going to win it does not matter who is in the plate. In my experience, this is true in some, but not most occasions, and a day seldom passes when I have not viewed a race and thought that the placings might have been different if the jockeys had been swapped.

I am going to make myself unpopular here but I believe it worth saying. There are too many jockeys scrapping over rides these days, especially in the south of England, and far too many of them rank between being barely competent and a liability to themselves and others. There may be twenty top jockeys who form the established nucleus. Then, each year, there will be a small group of talented youngsters beginning to make their way. Then come the cowboys.

There have always been bad jockeys going round but I feel the situation has deteriorated since the introduction of the conditional riders' scheme. It was the trainers who instigated that, for their own ends, and they must bear some of the responsibility for declining standards. Many trainers have made a practice of using youngsters only so long as they can claim seven pounds, lightening a horse's load. As soon as the kid rides enough winners to graduate to the senior school, the trainer kicks him out and finds another one with a claim. Discarded into the overcrowded jungle of freelances, the boy will then ride anything which comes along and try too hard to impress, which, mixed with limited ability, can be a very dangerous cocktail.

I wish there could be some method of sorting out the incompetents – some equivalent of a driving test – but I realise it is wishful thinking. The cowboys are with us to stay and, ruthless though it may sound, it is up to the better jockeys to apply the law of the jungle and keep them in their place.

Seniority does not make a jockey inviolate in the hurly burly of a race but it does gain him a certain amount of deference. If I am down at the start before a novice chase at Plumpton, to take the worst-case scenario, and the rest of the jockeys are all kids, claimers and amateurs, I will make it clear that I am going to sit second or third on the inside. Having said that, I will not brook any interference. Usually, there is none. Even the new-comers quickly learn where Scu, or Richard Dunwoody or I like to be in a race; they also learn that it is not in their long or short-term interests to mess us about.

Plenty know no better at first and will get in the way simply through clumsiness and over-enthusiasm. They are put straight with a few well-chosen words. If they do it again, it may become more serious. There is a ritualistic way among jockeys of sorting out scraps on the course. In the past, the days before stewarding vigilance was helped by modern technology, it was brutal; an offending jockey could be put through the wing of a fence for his sins. Some shocking injuries occurred that way and there might, in the modern age, be an ensuing charge of grievous bodily harm, hard though it would be to prove. Nowadays, such disagreements are sorted out in the weighing-room toilet, our equivalent of pistols at dawn.

It happens rarely, because it is a last resort, but it has happened to me four or five times during my career. Twice, however, I was so angered by what had happened during a race that it did not even reach the relative privacy of the loo.

The first occasion was a good few years ago now and concerned Craig Smith, who rode a lot of winners around the Midland tracks, especially for Martin Tate. We were in a race at Stratford and I know how long ago it must have been because I was riding a great old servant of Tom Jones's called The Sundance Kid.

Craig was in front as we turned the last bend into the straight but I knew my horse was going the better. Craig's was tiring and, as tired horses do, he drifted off the rails towards the centre of the course. In such circumstances I grabbed a perfectly acceptable chance to go past him on the inside but Craig, seeing me coming, steered his horse violently back to the left, chopping off my run.

We barged, bumped and cursed in pretty undignified style all the way to the last fence, where The Sundance Kid outjumped his opponent and went away to win. Neither of us was going to let the matter drop, though, and we snarled and swore at each other all the way back to the weighing-room. At that point, I told Craig to shut up or else. I had no clear idea what the 'all else' might be but I had had enough of the row, and after all, I had ridden a winner.

It was when he called me something obscene as he turned away that the red mists descended over me and I launched myself at him, landing a punch which caught him off balance and sent him flying through the swing doors of the weighing-room like in a scene from a Western. The stewards either didn't notice, or chose not to notice, and Craig and I later patched things up to become quite matey, but hitting another jockey is not something of which I am proud, and it was more than a decade before it happened again.

This time, the scene was Fakenham, that most rustic of courses up in north Norfolk. It was a Bank Holiday, I recall, and one of my rides was a mare called Duo Drom, trained by my erstwhile live-in lady, Di Haine. As on most Bank Holidays, jockey resources were stretched to the limit and it was not a particularly accomplished group which gathered down at the start. I made my intentions loudly clear, and wanted to stick to the inner for the good reason that the mare always drifted to the left. I was also intent on making the running to ensure a decent pace, as she probably wanted further than the two-mile trip, and I was duly at the head of affairs for the first of two circuits of Fakenham's tight, square-shaped track.

For a couple of hundred yards after jumping the last fence, there is no inside running rail. I kept a straight course for the point at which the rail resumes and I was not best pleased when I sensed one trying to cut off the corner and pass me on the inside. I spotted the distinctive green and white colours of Geoffrey Hubbard and knew they were being carried by a big Irish lad named Terry Barry, a seven-pound claimer who had joined the Hubbard yard after a spell with Jeff King. Half turning towards him, I told him not even to try it but he kept coming and coming until, with the rail only a few yards away, and my course as straight as it had always been, he had nowhere to go.

His primitive solution was to torpedo my horse, turning him sideways and costing me ground, momentum and temper.

I recovered to win the race easily enough but the public address was announcing a stewards' enquiry even as I pulled up. The dopey kid could hardly have chosen a worse place to carve me up, right under the stewards' box, and as we went to weigh in I told him bluntly what I thought of his intelligence.

It turned, I am afraid, into another ugly scene and I thought I was in trouble when I landed my best punch, right on his chin, and his only reaction was to shake his head. He was so much bigger than me that it would have been ruled a boxing mismatch but he made the mistake of lashing out at me with his boot. I caught his foot and twisted him to the floor, where he stayed until some of the other jockeys pulled us apart.

This may be a primitive means of resolving differences but there is no point in my trying to pretend it does not go on. Adrenalin flows freely during a race in which, not to be too melodramatic, we risk injury at every obstacle and every turn. It is a hard enough business without the knowing or witless interference of cowboys who have neither the brain nor the ability to sustain a career in the game.

It is, to my way of thinking, as manly a sport as there is. And that is why I have to say I am against lady jockeys competing against the men over jumps. I know I am inviting trouble here. I know I am a male chauvinist pig. But my opinions are genuinely held and, at least in part, they are caused by concern for the well-being of female bodies which were simply not made for the job.

If there was a way, amid the inevitable protests about women's rights, to confine the girl jockeys to their own races, it might be more acceptable. Nature did not design them to compete, on equal terms, against men in a sport where strength is a prerequisite.

Race-riding always has been dominated by males and, despite some well publicised successes for a few of the girls, that is the way it will continue to be. The girls will not get enough opportunities to make a living, because owners have to pay them the same as men, so they will always be doing no more than play at it.

The best of the girl jump jockeys have been Lorna Vincent and Gee Armytage. Both have struggled desperately to make a go of it and Lorna, I know, has several times been close to packing up. I admire her for her perseverance and she has shown, over the years, that certain horses will run for her. Both Lorna and Gee are better built for the job than many of the other girls, whose greatest danger is that they do not, or maybe cannot fall as men do. Eight out of ten falls can be controlled, the damage minimised by rolling into a ball. It is something I do instinctively but I have noticed, time after time, that the girl riders tend to just flop to the ground, doing themselves more initial harm and leaving themselves prone to kicks from following horses.

Chauvinist I may be, but I will also admit to a touch of concern for the girls. It is hard enough to jump a fence and find yourself galloping all over the prostrate body of a male jockey. When it is a girl, it turns my stomach.

Bluntly, I have never yet seen a girl jump jockey who is any better than a third-rate man. In general, they are more of a nuisance than a virtue and, because they will never compete on my terms, I would prefer it if they were not riding at all.

I have dealt, here, with some of the perennial problems confronting a jockey, from the suspicion of wrongdoing to the malice or incompetence of rival riders. Some jockeys, however, face the one insurmountable problem. It attacks when a career is past its sell-by date and, once under the skin, there is no treatment. When a jockey has lost his bottle, the only wise course is to pack up immediately.

There is a distinction, of course, between transient fear and the incurable condition which takes a jockey when his overwhelming concern is avoiding injury. If there is a jockey alive who can claim he has never been frightened in a race, I will show you either a fool or a liar. But gratifyingly few reach the stage where every ride is a trial, every fence a rigid exercise in self-preservation.

I have experienced fear, maybe half a dozen times in my career. To overcome it, on those rare occasions, I have channelled it into anger, with myself and with the horse. Then I put it out of my mind. If fear stays with you after a bad experience, or recurs in another race, your bottle is going and the way you have always ridden will change. You will know it straight away and those around you, the jockeys who ride with you day after day, will not take long to notice.

I was frightened when the reins snapped on that headstrong

two-mile chaser, Kyoto. And I was frightened at Plumpton one day when Eurolink Boy, a horse of Philip Mitchell's, was sent over fences for the first time. I had ridden him once over hurdles, and he was a pretty hairy ride then, but there had been no opportunity to school him over fences, a rare omission for me.

The value of the schooling grounds to the jockey, never mind the horse, was advertised luridly in this race. On the two-mile chase course at Plumpton, the first fence comes quickly and the next two are downhill. It is a trappy course which has disillusioned some distinguished jockeys in its time; the great Fred Winter, in his riding career, took a conscious decision never to go back there. But I have had plenty of success on the track and, so the trainer assured me, I could expect some more that afternoon.

Philip was right, but only after I had earned my riding fee and win percentage twice over. Eurolink took a fierce hold and, as we turned towards the first of the downhill fences he was charging at it like a five-furlong sprinter. All kinds of things can flash through a jockey's mind as he approaches a fence. In this case, there was no time for deep consideration, we were going too fast for that, but the one alarming fact in my head was that I had no idea what this horse was capable of. For all I knew, he might never have jumped a fence at home at all; I could not know whether he would pick up when I asked him, or plough straight through this notoriously unpopular fence, turn a double somersault and roll all over me. In those fleeting few seconds, I was scared.

It turned out well enough. He dived over that one and seemed to put on even more of a spurt going into the next. But he met that one OK, too, negotiated the sharp left-hand turn at the foot of the hill and began to come back under some sort of control. I won the battle with him and won the race, but it was not an experience I wanted to rapidly repeat.

There must have been other occasions but they are dismissed from the brain, better kept out of sight and mind. If it comes rarely, and passes quickly, a jockey is all right.

These days, not so many jockeys go on too long as did in the past. When I began, forty was an average age to be thinking of retirement. Nowadays, the competition is such that few are given the chance to go on that long; thirty-five is a more usual age for packing up, and I have surprised myself by riding on past that mark.

I hope, when the time comes, that I don't have to be told to go. I hope I get out with my bottle intact, or at least when I first experience the warning signs. I don't think I could stand to be scrutinised, as I have scrutinised old jockeys in the past, and for colleagues to tell each other that the old Eck has lost his bottle.

Chapter Eleven

The title of champion jockey never did come my way and now, I accept, it never will. Only a rider with relentless ammunition provided by the likes of Martin Pipe or, in Richard Dunwoody's case, a combination of two top trainers, can have serious hopes of the championship. The rest of us have to look to maintain a regular flow of winners, with hopefully the occasional big one among them. Each season, I have set myself an initial target of fifty winners, a benchmark if you like, and in the last dozen years or so I have not often fallen below that standard unless injuries have badly interfered. It is also true, though, that I have never exceeded the mark by much. I have been consistent all right but, in looking back, I admit there have been times when I was also complacent, when the appetite and ambition was replaced by a cocksure certainty that things would fall into my lap. In those years, I imagine I was a difficult bloke to work with and live with.

The personal side of my life was settled, if not always steady, for most of the 1980s. I spent eight years with the same woman and assumed that it would always be that way. But time, the clash of personalities and perhaps my own insatiable wanderlust got the better of that, too. As I write, I am a bachelor again, poorer, wiser and happier for it.

The long-term relationship was in some ways a remarkable coincidence, though at the time it seemed more like a natural progression. The girl involved was Tom Jones's daughter, Di, and it came about because her own marriage, to the former jockey Johnny Haine, broke up and she came back to the

Newmarket area from Gloucestershire. Di moved in to a house in the village of Malton; right next door, Mr and Mrs Smith Eccles were in the process of dissolving their very brief marriage.

There was nothing in it at first. I knew Di well enough, of course, from my apprentice years, but the extent of our early contact was confined to her asking me to baby-sit with her two kids if she wanted to go out on a summer evening. I obliged happily enough and, as time passed, we began to book an outside baby-sitter and go out together.

We moved in together in the village of Snailwell. It was a lovely old house with a big garden, in which I happily pottered around on free days. There were stables attached and, although Di was working quite successfully in the bloodstock business – at the time, a more thriving industry than it is now – I encouraged her to think about setting up as a trainer. With her contacts in one area of the horse business, and mine in another, I was confident that we could attract enough good owners to establish a competitive yard. We were both experienced enough to be aware of the pitfalls and to know our limitations. I had faith in Di's knowledge and drive, and naturally I reasoned that setting up the yard when we did would give me a ready-made future when I stopped riding.

We never seriously discussed how it would work out when that day came, whether the licence would pass into my name or whether Di would continue as the licence-holder with my unnamed assistance. The mechanics scarcely mattered; it was just accepted that, one way or another, we would run the yard together.

To some degree, it was like that from the start. It is not a straightforward business, setting up as a trainer, and it hardly matters who you are, people are not immediately going to patronise you in droves. Even John Francome found that out. But we did pick up some nice horses and some good owners, some from Di's circle and some from mine. She attacked the new job with great determination and I supported it as best I could, doing all the schooling of the horses and riding out on days when I did not have to school elsewhere. We had planted a few acorns, but the initial signs of growth were very encouraging. The occasional horse was proving good enough to run at the festivals, and Qannas, a particularly nice type of stayer, winning four times in a season. New owners were gradually being drawn in and the venture was paying its way.

My partnership with Di, however, was a combustible one and the explosions were frequent. She is a very strong character, as one would expect from her parentage, and when teamed up with my tendency to say and do exactly what I think, the potential for damaging storms was ever present. We survived eight years, but I sometimes wonder how.

I don't believe I was ever one to bring the job home with me and brood. I know jockeys who habitually do this – by his own admission, Peter Scudamore used to be a prime example – but, although my moods do reflect my job, I seldom dwell on a day's work, good or bad. If a couple of favourites have been beaten, I've had a painful fall and the stewards have had me in for a whip offence I will briefly be grouchy. If I had a cat I might kick it. But a few minutes in the armchair with a glass of scotch will invariably restore the Eccles equilibrium. The opposite scenario has no greater effect on me. If I have ridden a big winner, I don't hang on to the elation. Tomorrow can bring the losers and the falls.

So, in terms of my riding, I think my feet were firmly on the ground during this period. Arguably, too firmly. I had a nice house, a ready-made family, fast car and enough money to sustain the lifestyle of my choice. The future seemed likely to take care of itself so why should I worry? I think I began to coast, dangerously so, and if there were few outward signs of it in my riding, perhaps my attitude betrayed it. I had come up the hard way, with nothing laid on a plate and no silver spoon to eat it with. I had always needed to graft and now, because it seemed that was no longer the case, the motivation of the real me had receded.

Not that I had become a guy for the slippers and pipe. Far from it. I was still playing as hard as ever, in social terms, and some of my escapades were probably not designed to endear me to those closest to me. Just occasionally, however, I was an innocent victim. I think the infamous Aintree kidnap was one such episode.

In hindsight, the one real mistake I made during that regrettable business was in going on television to tell the story. It did not change what had happened, and that in itself was appalling enough, but it portrayed me to everyone listening – and that inevitably included some pretty influential people in the racing world – as a desperado, irresponsible at best and unprofessional at worst. The thing had developed out of trouble with Di but the self-publicity I unthinkingly gave it created trouble on other fronts, too.

Let me explain. It was April 1986. I was nearing the end of perhaps the best season of my career. See You Then had won his second Champion Hurdle and I had never been out of the top three in the jockeys' table. I was flying, and there was still the big Liverpool meeting to look forward to. See You Then was chalked down to run, and so was River Ceiriog, surprise winner of the Supreme Novices Hurdle at Cheltenham. Kathies Lad would try to win the Captain Morgan two-mile chase for the second consecutive year and, in the Grand National itself, Nick Henderson's Classified gave me as good a winning opportunity as I have ever had in the race. All this, and the annual social merry-go-round of Liverpool, to boot. But it was that, or the lack of it, which was my undoing.

I have always loved the Liverpool meeting. The racing itself has been steadily upgraded over the years, so that the supporting cards are now of a very high quality. The racecourse, too, has undergone regular improvements. It remains, however, a week which revolves around the one spectacular event, just before four o'clock on the Saturday afternoon. Everything else is the warm-up, the entire week a steady gathering of tension and anticipation for the race which is uniquely Aintree, inimitably British.

The Irish have never come to Aintree in the same numbers as they do for Cheltenham, but their leading jockeys are almost always present and, as is their wont, they plunge enthusiastically into the after-hours entertainment. For some years, I used to spend the three days at the Holiday Inn in Liverpool, where the company was always riotous. I often wondered why the Irish bothered to book rooms, so seldom did they use them, and I have a particular memory of coming down at seven o'clock one morning and finding the great Tommy Carberry still at the bar, the latest of innumerable pints of Guinness in front of his smiling face.

I had a lot of fun at the Holiday Inn but it was dangerous territory – there was no chance of slipping off for an early night with the likes of Carberry and Tommy McGivern about. In 1986, I decided to abandon the pleasures of Irish company and alcoholic nights; Di and I decided we would stay, instead, up the coast at Southport, in the anachronistic Royal Clifton Hotel. Recent improvements have not entirely removed the air of a dated and dowdy seaside hotel from this place, but it is undoubtedly friendly and, I thought, less likely to get me into any trouble before the important rides in my book. There were also enough racing people staying in Southport to ensure we would not exactly be lonely, and we set off on the Thursday morning with spirits and expectations high.

In this game, things very seldom turn out the way you expect but of all the unpredictable things which have befallen me over the years I think the events of that meeting will live with me the longest. I had the best National ride of my life, discovering the heady, unforgettable thrill which comes from a belief, sustained over almost the entire four-and-a-half miles, that the world's most famous race can be yours. But the hurdle races I expected to win were both lost, I fell out badly with Di and spent a night in my car which was not as lonely, and far more exciting, than I had planned.

It all came about because I reacted uncharacteristically badly to a losing ride. I had considered River Ceiriog a banker for the opening day, after the style in which he had spreadeagled an apparently stronger field of novices at Cheltenham, and when he was turned over by I Bin Zaidoon, one of the horses which were bringing Terry Ramsden to such prominence at that time, I was as close to inconsolable as I have ever been over a race. The scotch bottle was summoned for liberal consolation, I am afraid, but it did nothing to lighten my mood and, by the time I had found my solitary way back to Southport, the idea of a quiet meal with Di had no appeal. I told her so, rudely and bluntly, and her justifiable response was to say I could find somewhere else to spend the night. We parted to a percussion of oaths and slammed doors and I broodily linked up with some old friends, and more old whisky, before trying to make the most of a bad job and climbing into the back of my Mercedes.

Blame the booze, the strains of the day or sheer fatigue, but it seems I made the elementary mistake of leaving the car keys in the ignition before curling up under a blanket on the capacious back seat. There were few street lights to illuminate the car, where it was parked, and the thief-cum-joyrider who chanced upon it some time later must have thought all his birthdays had come at once. He did not pass up the gift, and so it was that I awoke from a deep sleep wondering first where on earth I was and then, with that hazily recalled, why I appeared to be moving.

I sat up abruptly, in the way you do when awaking from a nightmare. But it was no dream, I discovered. This was real and frightening. I was being driven in my own car, I knew not where or by whom. Whoever it was, and he turned out to be a teenager, had not bargained on company and his reaction was, in hindsight, quite amusing – a strangled scream of terror, a jab at the brakes, a skid onto the hard shoulder and retreat, at a run, without so much as a formal introduction.

It did not occur to me at the time that I had just enjoyed a very lucky escape. My unwitting kidnapper had been young, naive and alone. If he had been a serious criminal, and in company, the career of S. Smith Eccles might have come to an end in a way bizarre enough to tax the combined brains of Inspectors Wexford and Morse for a good few episodes. As it was, I had suffered nothing more grievous than a fright and, although in no state to be driving along the motorways of Merseyside, I managed to navigate back to Southport sea front, re-park the car and grab another few hours of rest, this time with the doors locked and the keys in my pocket. It could have been a lot worse.

Daylight brought a clearer awareness of what I had been through and I am afraid I succumbed to human nature. Certain aspects of the story were embarrassing but it was an unquestionably good tale, the sort which people hear related with that irreconcilable mix of alarm and envy. I couldn't wait to tell someone about it and, after the discreet but agog attentions of my valet, John Buckingham, I became less choosy about who heard it. Inevitably, word soon spread to the BBC TV team, who thought it was a must for their audience. The thing was now running out of control but, unable or unwilling to foresee that not everyone would think it all a great laugh, I ploughed on, still enjoying the limelight of notoriety.

All such smugness had long gone by the time I woke up to the newspaper headlines on Grand National day. I featured in most of them – it was heaven-sent copy for the hacks – and by now I was aware that there were those for whom I rode whose opinion of me had sharply lowered. Thinking about it more logically, I could well see why. Here I was, attached to one of the most prestigious stables in the land – Nick, in fact, was about to be champion trainer – and in the middle of one of the season's most important meetings I was getting drunk, sleeping rough in a car and inviting the criminal elements of Southport to do their worst with me. Just as indictable, in some eyes, was the way in which I had apparently bragged about it on TV. Nick had already made his feelings known, provoked I think by his owners as much as any personal animosity, and as Saturday dawned, I knew with an uncomfortable certainty that my riding would be scrutinised closer than ever before, plenty just waiting to pounce on any sign of being below my best for unacceptable reasons.

In fact I was bright, in mind and body if not in spirit. With Di still frosty, the funny side of the kidnap having passed her by, too, I had spent a chaste and simple night in a different hotel, featuring a quiet meal and about ten hours' sleep. I went out and won on Kathies Lad, which eased the pressure a little, but I was only due for another setback and it came through the defeat of See You Then. It was not down to me, and to be fair no one suggested it was, but the circumstances were such that I felt the world was conspiring against me. I needed something special in the National and, thanks to Classified, I got it.

Classified was a specialist two-and-a-half-mile horse but experience had proved that this gave him no less chance of winning a National than the thorough, dogged stayer. He was an athlete, a very safe jumper, and he had shown he could handle Aintree by finishing fifth in the race the previous year, when ridden by John White. My ride that season, Hill of Slane, had fallen, a fate with which I was familiar. Of six previous rides in the race, I had completed the course only once. But Classified filled me with hope; he had been trained specifically for the National and Nick felt he had never been better. He was right.

I think I had become ambivalent about the National. It came from too many disappointments, of course, too many years when the anticipation was not remotely matched by the reality. But Classified altered all that, giving me a ride I shall never forget.

He was pretty much foot perfect all the way round, took the lead on jumping Bechers for the second time and, although running out of gas to allow West Tip and Young Driver the finish between them, finished a gallant third.

Nick was beaming, wide-eyed with excitement and pleasure. For a while, the traumas of the week were filed away. This, after all, was just the latest in a long line of great days we had enjoyed together and, if his long-standing reservations about my approach had inevitably been reinforced by the controversies of the week, we were still a good and successful team which we both wanted to keep intact.

Once the euphoria of the National ride abated, however, I was left with a lot of patching-up to do. First Di, then Nick and his owners. Neither mission was easily accomplished but Di and I, having settled our difference when I went home on the Sunday, presented a united front for dinner with the Hendersons at the end of the week. Nick and I retired to the study with a drink to talk things through and, to put things simply, I apologised for being irresponsible and he accepted on the tacit understanding that he would not support me if anything similar should ever occur.

The good times rolled again. River Ceiriog restored his reputation by going to Ayr and winning the Scottish Champion Hurdle, a great day on which Nick and I were thoroughly spoiled, flat-racing style, by travelling in a private plane belonging to the horse's owner, Bobby McAlpine. Then, the following year, despite the heartbreak over See You Then, we won a second Triumph Hurdle together with Alone Success. Nick was champion trainer for the second successive year and I topped fifty winners again; Windsor House was home to some of the best horses in the country and most jockeys would have been thinking of seeing out their career there, given half a chance.

Whether the chance was there for me to do so, I doubt. Nick, as was only right, had his eyes on the future and felt he ought to be engaging a jockey on a long-term basis as I was unlikely to go on much longer. There were days when I probably did not discourage such a view, when a quiet life training a few jumpers with Di seemed a soft option. And then, as ever, there was my gypsy spirit to contend with. The upshot of it all was that Nick and I once again agreed to separate. There was no anger, no acrimony and regrettably little sadness. We just drifted apart, just as I have drifted in and out of jobs throughout my career. We have remained friends, indeed we get along better now than ever before, and I have never entirely stopped riding a few for him. But Nick linked up with Jamie Osborne, then with Richard Dunwoody, while I returned to my roots as a freelance. Life became tougher again, complacency was banished. It saved my career, then prolonged it.

Oddly enough, the split in my personal life, separation from Di Haine, was also responsible in no small part for my continued presence among the declared riders. The training option vanished, along with my home and much of my security, and for the past couple of years I have had to scrap for everything again. It has been more like the old Eck, and I have found myself easier to live with.

I have rediscovered the fun of the lifestyle. It may not have the same social life as it once did, and there is certainly far less in the way of mixing over a few drinks, but the game has plenty of laughs, on and off the course, such as the day at Fontwell, a few seasons back, when the new, inquiring SIS cameras caught me in a compromising position.

It was my first ride for a few days and I had put on a pound or two too many. Saunas have always repelled me and so, as a last resort, I turned to what we jockeys know as the pee-pill, which releases enough fluid from the body to make the difference in a tight situation with the scales. That, anyway, is the theory, but, it being my first time, I did not know the practice, which is that the pill must be taken at breakfast-time to have its full effect. I had taken it, in my glib innocence, only two hours before racing, and as we waited to weigh out, I had still not passed water and, consequently, had to ride at a pound overweight.

I was well past the point of no return when it happened, down at the start and circling with the other runners. But when the pill does take effect, there is nothing to be done about it. You just have to pee. To the bewilderment of everyone else, I jumped off my horse, handed the reins to one of the starter's assistants and galloped down to what I imagined was the relative privacy behind the first fence, where, after what seemed an eternity, I gained great and prolonged relief. What I did not know was that a bored cameraman had turned his attentions to this figure with his breeches round his ankles and the incident was duly recorded for posterity – and many subsequent re-runs.

If wasting for rides is one perennial moan of my breed, another is the travelling. I know everyone has to get to work and few people enjoy their journey, be it by car, train or on foot. But I venture to suggest the jump jockey has it particularly tough in this respect. He does a lot of his travelling in the worst weather of the year and, for most of us, an hour on the road each way is a luxury – many times it can be three each way. Unlike our counterparts on the flat, flying is usually out of the equation, so our cars get a fair old hammering during a season.

I like fast cars and have been fortunate to own my share. I have grown accustomed to driving alone, usually with Radio One blaring on the stereo speakers for company. I have perfected my own network of routes to and from racecourses and I am inclined to cut them down to the shortest possible journey time. My bugbear is the West Midlands courses – Bangor, Hereford, Ludlow and even Worcester, because there is no easy route and I will do well to escape with only six hours' driving when I ride at any of them. So it was that, one Saturday in August after evening racing at Worcester, I was making good speed through the village of Alcester just as darkness had begun to fall. I do not normally stop for hitch-hikers but the willowy blonde waving her thumb at me from the pavement looked too good an invitation to pass up. I was driving a Porsche and prepared to turn on the charm, a mode I hastily revised when the blonde settled daintily into the passenger seat and then turned to face me. It had, I consoled myself been a mistake anyone might have made but, at close quarters, there was absolutely no doubt. This was no sexy young lady, but a bloke in drag!

Amid the good times and the funny times were some bleak spells, too. I only rode thirty winners in 1987–88, a good start being sabotaged by a long spell on the injury list. I fell five short of my fifty-winner target the next year but, in 1989–90, I rode fifty-six at a strike-rate of better than a winner every four rides. Only Scu, with Martin Pipe's winner's machine behind him, could better that.

When the new season began in August 1990, I had only the usual, realistic aims. I had no retainers, no leading trainer backing me, just a steady stream of competitive rides to anticipate. No one was more surprised than I when my first nine rides of the season all won, putting me on the brink of the all-time record of ten.

It had been, in most ways, a predictably quiet start to a season. A dry summer had left the ground firm, too firm for most trainers to risk their horses. The way was clear for the fast-ground specialists to mop up and I did not think I had many of them to ride. Well, I didn't, but the nine I rode during the first three weeks of the season were all good enough to beat some pretty poor opposition. No one sets out to run up that sort of sequence. At that time of year, a jockey is just grateful to get on a few horses with a winning chance. And it was not as if I had suddenly achieved great popularity among trainers. Between 4 August and 25 August, I rode at nine different meetings, with only one booked ride on each occasion.

All the races were over hurdles and almost all of my rides were favourite. The longest-priced winner was 5–4 against and, in all, I beat a total of only thirty horses. If this puts the saga in some sort of perspective, it may also explain why I did not subscribe to the growing sense of media excitement – at least, not until I rode the ninth, and stood on the threshold of a spot of history.

Frankie Durr, one-time jockey and successful trainer on the flat, turned his hand to a bit of jumping that year and his early-season types, all fit from the flat, were well worth riding. He started me off with an odds-on shot at Market Rasen, though I only got him home by a short-head. The next five winners were easier. I won by a distance on Chucklestone at Newton Abbot and when his trainer, Jeff King, turned him out again at Devon three days later, the opposition was all scared off and we had a walkover. I then won two more for Jeff with scarcely more effort than the walkover, before Gavin Pritchard-Gordon had his first runner of the season, back at Fontwell. This horse was called Spofforth and was to be central to the story. He won his debut by twenty lengths and, returning to Fontwell eight days later, won another juvenile hurdle with a bit in hand. In between times, Frankie Durr had turned out One for the Boys to win at Market Rasen and, on 25 August, the same horse on the same course beat four moderate rivals to put me on nine out of nine.

Now, I had to give the matter some thought. The press had

seized upon the record attempt and I was endlessly taking calls asking me where I would be going on the Monday to try for double figures. Monday happened to be a Bank Holiday and, although various trainers were now willing to put me up on supposed 'good things', I had no hesitation in going down to Plumpton. For the first time since the season began, I had two rides rather than one and, as things turned out, only the planning of the card cost me a share of the record. The weather was good and the crowd was among the biggest seen for years on this little, hilly Sussex track. It was a pleasant setting, if not a prestigious one, and with a battery of TV cameramen and photographers following me about, I felt quite a celebrity for a day. In the knowledge that two winners would give me the record outright, I also felt justified in confidence.

My first ride was the aptly named Vision of Wonder. Trained by Jeff King, he had beaten a solitary opponent to win his previous race in bloodless style and was sent off the 8–11 favourite in a field of four. But the vision faded, and with it the wonder and the glory. I came to take up the running between the last two flights and still thought I would win jumping the last. But I was passed on the run-in and beaten four lengths – ironically, by a horse which had not run for ten months, finished lame and has never run again. It is typical of jump racing that history should be mocked and defied by an unfancied semi-cripple on borrowed time.

Spofforth, my second ride, won an eight-runner novice event by ten lengths. He would, wouldn't he. Still, ten out of eleven was the sort of start I could not have dreamed about a month earlier. I was in the news again, set up for the season, and as the consoling murmurs of 'bad luck' and 'good try' continued all day and into the next, it occurred to me that other people were far more disappointed for me than I was for myself.

Chapter Twelve

Sir Piers Bengough, KCVO, OBE, is one of the most distinguished figures in the racing industry. In twenty-one years
of riding as an amateur he won the Grand Military at Sandown
four times. Then, as if by prior arrangement, he became a
member, and a steward of the Jockey Club. He is the Queen's
representative at Ascot and a director of three other jumping
courses. He is accustomed to exerting authority. So when, behind
closed doors at Portman Square, late in 1991, Sir Piers suggested
to me that it was time I hung up my boots, it was not the sort
of throwaway comment I could easily laugh off.

The circumstances were unpleasant, even before this cutting
aside. Putting a complicated matter as simply as possible, I stood
accused on two counts. Those outside racing alleged that I was
guilty of cruelty; those within the sport might have known better,
but still had me tried, essentially for incautious and misleading
remarks liable to bring racing into disrepute.

It was a mess. A depressing mess. What is worse, it came from
the latest winner of a season which was shaping up into my
most promising for some years. I had won the big hurdle at
Cheltenham's Mackeson meeting on Sally Oliver's Shu Fly and I
had won three races on two exciting young chasers called Keep
Talking and Norman Conqueror, both trained by Tim Thomson
Jones for Jim Joel. The second win on Norman Conqueror,
earlier in the week concerned, had earned me the sort of rave
reviews in the papers which took me back ten years, to the days
when I was thrusting my way towards senior status aboard The

Sundance Kid and Tingle Creek. I was going well, and enjoying every minute.

Saturday 23 November carried the hint of further spoils. Newcastle is not exactly on the doorstep and there have been many times when I might have resented the need to travel to the far north-east instead of riding at Newbury's Hennessy Gold Cup day. But my rides at Gosforth Park that afternoon included Fidway, who, I remain convinced, might well have given me a fourth Champion Hurdle the previous March but for unseating me when cruising at the third last. He was bound to need this first outing of a new season but, in addition, I had two rides for Denys Smith, an experienced and accomplished trainer in the north who had begun to use my services only a few weeks earlier.

One of the Smith runners was Ballinrostig, a giant of a staying chaser with whom I had begun to strike up a good relationship. He blew up when I first rode him at Wetherby but showed me enough to know he had plenty of ability. Enough, anyway, to persuade me to miss another Newbury card and drive all the way to Kelso, in the Scottish Borders, during the first week of November. He lost out by a neck there, to one of Gordon Richards' vast string of chasers, but both Denys and I retained great faith in him and he was due to run in a field of six for a three-mile handicap. I thought he would win.

It was not a straightforward proposition, however, because Ballinrostig was so well handicapped that he had only nine stone four pounds in the race. No horse can carry less than ten stone, so he was automatically burdened with ten pounds more than his official assessment, and it is a good few years since I rode at ten stone, or anything near. I half expected Denys to put up someone else, on the basis that he could not afford to run his horse from out of the handicap and put up extra overweight, but he judged that I knew Ballinrostig, and that the horse was the sort who needed strong handling. Gratefully, I retained the ride and set about getting down to as light a weight as possible.

I managed 10–5, which entailed a diet of fresh air for twenty-four hours before the race. If, as is quite possible, this left me a shade weak and short of energy, it might help explain what happened when I got off the horse after the race.

It must have been a good race to watch and, fortunately for them, Channel Four cameras were there to cover it. Ballinrostig is a big strong sort and, three fences from home, he began to hang right-handed. He kept jumping well enough, though, and responded to all my urgings, running on gamely from the front and holding Nos Na Gaoithe by three lengths. A few yards after the line his stride shortened and I knew he was lame; in the accepted way, I immediately jumped off him and prepared to lead him, hobbling, back to the winner's enclosure, a sad way for any winner to be acclaimed. I was exhausted, partly through the wasting and partly through the rigours of the ride. I knew I had been hard on him but I also knew it had been necessary. A couple of times, I had used the whip down his shoulder to straighten him up; if I had not, he would probably have run out. From the second last, I hit him regularly, but not with undue violence, simply to do my job and get the most out of a horse for himself and his connections. I thought I had done the job well. Jim McGrath, on Channel Four, was just telling his viewers as much, adding that he thought those who had backed him were indebted to me for drawing the money. It was at this point that Jim handed over to Derek Thompson and the day began to turn sour.

Derek is a friend of mine and I bear him no ill will at all for what occurred. He was only doing his job. The fault lay with a system which could allow a tired jockey, with his blood up and his thoughts jumbled, to be interviewed on the course before he had even been able to discuss the race with his owners and trainer. It was patently wrong and, as a direct result of this incident, it can no longer happen. The ban, however, came too late to help me.

I was breathing hard when the microphone was put under my nose and Derek asked a perfectly innocent question about the race. My reply was misguided in the extreme. As was clear to anyone who has ever ridden a horse, it was also impossibly confused. What I actually said was that this was a very brave horse 'because he went lame three out'. What I should have said, and what really happened, was that he had begun to hang three fences out. He simply would not have jumped the last three if he had broken down already, and I know of no jockey mad enough, let alone cruel enough, to fire a horse into a fence, with all its attendant risks, if he thought he was lame.

But it was said. Television is an instant medium and I could not take it back if I wanted to. At the time, what with trying to get my own breath back and to deal with my limping partner, I did not give it another thought. It did not entirely surprise me when I was called before the stewards and, although I thought it rough justice, they were technically within their rights when they stood me down for four days on a whip offence. It was much later, when my TV comment began to get around, that the real trouble began.

There was no problem, then or later, with either Denys Smith or the owners. They all accepted the sad fact that jumpers do break down and, although the horse was ruled out for the rest of the season, he had at least gone out with a win. He was only eight years old and they could expect more from him when the leg recovered. I hoped I might ride him again and nobody told me otherwise.

No, it was not the connections who took issue with me. It was the RSPCA and, worthy though their intentions are, I knew at once that they could make an unfair bundle of trouble for me. Naturally, they seized on my words, took them at face value and painted me as some sort of ogre. In time, they sought and received permission to go and see the horse. They could find, of course, no evidence of damage from my whip, but by then they had done their own sort of damage – to my reputation.

It is not pleasant for a jockey to find himself portrayed as cruel. By definition, jockeys spend much of their lives in company with horses and, for all that we might treat the job as a business, an affection for the animals is natural. I love horses as much as anyone else in the sport and I would never knowingly cause one any distress. The allegations being made against me now were plain ludicrous but, as happens in such cases, I had no means of defence. The letters were the worst thing. Some were angry, some abusive, all painfully personal and most cowardly in their anonymity. A man has no right of reply when he does not know who it is that accuses him, and I felt a mixture of depression that anyone could feel such things about me, and anger that they should hide from a reaction. I don't doubt that there were plenty in racing who assumed I would feel nothing, that I would breeze through the episode in my familiar cavalier style. Well, they were wrong. It got to me in a big way, especially when the Jockey Club informed me that I was to appear before them to explain the incident. They did add that I was facing no specific charges and that the inquiry was designed only to clarify the facts, but this did not stop the media speculating and nor did it stop my own brain working overtime as to what could now befall me. The powers of the Jockey Club stewards are almost unlimited and, although I could not envisage they had any grounds for suspending me further, or even revoking my licence to ride, I was not in the mood for complacency.

Inside Portman Square, things can be rather intimidating. A jockey who has to appear at HQ will arrive in trepidation and, if he has any sense, conduct himself with due deference. Proceedings are formal and there is seldom any idle conversation. Which is why, when Sir Piers dropped his bombshell, I knew he was making a serious point.

I had been through the affair in great detail once again, explaining exactly why I said the fateful words to Derek Thompson and why, during the race itself, I had to be firm with the horse. The stewards listened politely, of course, but I had the suspicion they were not convinced, a feeling borne out when Sir Piers asked me if I was thinking of retiring shortly.

Slightly in shock, I asked him what he meant. He said that when jockeys reach a certain age and lose their natural fitness, the first thing they do is resort to the whip. He could hardly have been more pointed as to what he thought of the incident, nor more transparent as to his views on my future. If he was not exactly instructing me to hang up my boots, he was certainly suggesting it as a good idea. I stood there wondering if they had the power to take it a stage further and insist but, indignation winning through, I told Sir Piers that in my opinion I was riding as well as ever, if not better, and that I had no plans to give up in the foreseeable future.

The inquiry ended inconclusively, so far as I was concerned. As they had promised, there were no charges and no additional punishment, but neither was there any hint of vindication for me. It was a case of the Jockey Club being seen to have done the right thing; I was left to stew in my misery. I felt a little resentful about the public nature of it all, felt that any words the stewards needed to have with me could equally well have taken place in private.

In the feudal world of racing, however, it is not a jockey's place to question the authority of the stewards. Our livelihood is in their hands and can, at any time, be taken away. The fact that I had apparently even put that thought in the head of a steward left me pretty shaken, and a season which had promised so much was never the same again. Over the New Year period I was unseated from fancied horses three times in consecutive days. Adding injury to insult was the last straw. The third unseating broke my ankle and, despite two vain attempts at a comeback, I was destined to miss some choice rides at Cheltenham.

I could hardly blame the stewards for that and, on calmer reflection I was prepared to concede that they were only acting in what they saw as the best interests of racing's image. As jockeys, we all fall foul of the stewards now and again but I am not about to join the chorus of those who believe them blinkered or overtly reactionary. Consistency may be lacking among stewards from one course to another but the intention is usually correct. I number stewards among my personal friends, indeed, and more than once I have had to stifle a grin when standing in front of a chap with whom I might have had too much scotch only a few days earlier. They have a job to do, just as we jockeys do, and there are instances when theirs is no easier. The whip rule, as it stands, leaves both jockeys and stewards with a dilemma. There is a guideline that no horse should be hit more than ten times. Recently, I was suspended for four days after just one blow too many. I was on a lazy horse in a tight finish. I believe I would have lost the race if I had put the stick down sooner. So where are a jockey's priorities – to his owners and trainer, who engage him, pay the bills and have a right to expect him to try his hardest to win on their horse, or to an ambiguous rule which, literally applied to certain situations, can be translated as saying you should not try to win if it means exceeding the stated dose. There is a lot of whip abuse in the sport and it can be unsightly. I hate seeing a beaten horse hit, and there are times when I have seen some cowboy or other thrashing a weary animal to try and finish sixth rather than seventh. This is the sort of thing which must be outlawed, rather than the occasions when a jockey is riding out his horse with a genuine chance of winning the race, using the whip correctly. The media, however, have overplayed the problem and the Jockey Club has been over-sensitive to it. The result is a situation, equally applicable to flat and jumping, when a jockey can find himself liable to censure whatever he does – either excessive use, or failing to ride out his horse in an attempt to win. As we are all paid to win races, and without that instinct we would not be doing the job, a great deal more are punished for whip offences than for giving up, whatever the impoverished punter may think!

My own view on this is that the ten strokes guideline, now further reduced to five, should be abandoned as it serves only to confuse an already fraught subject. Each case should be dealt with independently, at the discretion of the stewards; in this way, perhaps, the unsightly butchers can be weeded out, while the strong finishers are left alone.

I have always been regarded as a strong rider but I would refute any suggestion that I am indiscriminate with the whip. In common with most young jockeys, I am sure I was over-enthusiastic at times in my early days but I believe I am sensible now, and although I do find myself in the stewards' room, maybe once or twice a season, it is as much my vigorous style which attracts attention as any excessive belabouring of a horse.

So the whip rule is one thing I would sort out if I were senior steward for a day. Another would be to address the farce which goes by the name of race planning. I am sure those currently responsible for fixing the programme of meetings, and the races therein, must have a strong sense of humour. Nothing else could explain the number of absurd anomalies.

Recently, for instance, there were three jump meetings on an October Friday, at Newbury, Hereford and Exeter – all three in the south-west quarter of the country. Yet on the Mondays before and after that Friday, there were no jump meetings scheduled at all. I am aware that there are persuasive local reasons why certain courses cannot or will not stage meetings on certain days but this seems to be taking flexibility too far.

From a jockeys' viewpoint, it is also irritating to have a week in which Newton Abbot stage a meeting on the Monday, Tuesday's card might be at Market Rasen and Wednesday back down to Devon for the Exeter track. Here, I may be speaking through the overworked tyres of my car, but it seems a nonsense all the same.

Every trainer has his individual complaint about planning, usually on grounds such as the staging of three two-mile handicap chases on the same day and no others for a week. Trainers, like jockeys, will complain about whatever most inconveniences them. That is human nature. But there is no dispute, within all of us who work at this game every day, that the planning is inconsistent and unprofessional. Something ought to be done.

Not all racing officials come under the Smith Eccles hammer. Far from it. There are some highly skilled men working in the management of racecourses these days and, if their ranks are still undermined by the odd incompetent, well, the same can be said for virtually every profession. I also have plenty of time for the men who work, day by day, on the racecourses, often in the worst of weather. Groundstaff have my admiration; so, too, the men who work down at the start, especially the stalls-handlers on flat tracks, who take their life into their hands every time they have to deal with some ignorant, reluctant animal.

One breed which comes in for its share of abuse from jockeys is the clerks of the scales. Here again, personal interest prevails. The man who sits in judgement on the scales is unlikely to be a jockey's best friend, because it is in front of this man's eagle eyes that the results of several day's wasting are judged and, it must be said, where one or two other common dodges may be discovered.

Cheating the scales has been a commonplace occurrence among jump jockeys ever since I have been riding. Some of my best friends, John Francome and Ian Watkinson among them, have made an art form of it, frequently passing the scales far lighter than they will actually ride but returning to weigh in, innocent smile in place, with excess equipment discarded and the correct weight magically restored. Watty needed all his cunning in this direction because he was so heavily built and frequently took rides at way below his natural weight. This was widely known among the clerks, of course, but it was one thing to be aware that Watty was up to something and quite another to identify which device he was using from his box of tricks. One particularly vigilant clerk, by the name of Hopkins, took it upon himself to get to the bottom of it.

One of Ian's favourite 'props' was a pair of what he called cheating boots, which were no thicker than leather socks. One day at Stratford Mr Hopkins asked Watty if he intended to ride in them. What he actually intended to do was change into something much stronger – and heavier – before going out to the parade ring but Mr Hopkins was a shrewd old guy and he initialled the sole of the boots, telling Ian he would check them again when he weighed in. Without an alternative, Ian simply had to ride in them and, despite putting racecards inside for extra protection, he came back with his feet bruised and bleeding.

Another day at Wolverhampton, it was Ian's turn to put one over on old Hopkins, though it was a close-run thing. He had agreed to ride a very dodgy character called Hopeful Hill, who had been to the races four times previously that season, each time with a different jockey and each time failing to start. He was so mulish that the Jockey Club was considering warning him off. The trainer told Ian he had ten stone two pounds but finally agreed that he could put up five pounds overweight. Ian cheated like hell to get through, swapping boots and saddle for heavier items before going out to ride, confident in the belief that Hopeful Hill would not set off and so he would not be required to weigh in.

I can imagine Ian's horror when the horse, whom he had allowed to stand still at the start, encouraging his mulishness, shot away from the tapes into a clear lead, jumping enthusiastically. Turning into the straight, he was forced to think quickly. Hopeful Hill was not going to win, nor even be placed, but if he completed the course there was still a danger that Ian would be asked to weigh in, his excess pounds inevitably discovered, disciplinary action almost certain. And so, after jumping the last, Ian pulled the horse up, jumped off and inspected a hind leg as if fearful he had broken down. Then he walked the horse past the post, breezed back into the weighing room and confidently called 'pulled up' to Mr Hopkins. Easy, if you have the front for it!

One of a jockey's private dreads is forgetting to weigh in after he has won, or been placed, in a race. The procedure is that the clerk of the scales then lodges an objection which, when sustained, leads to automatic disqualification. This is costly and annoying enough for the offending jockey, but he then has to go through the embarrassment of explaining himself to the horse's owners, who may have been into the second bottle of champagne when the chilling announcement came across the public address.

Some famous names have fallen foul of this system but the trainer, John Jenkins, tells of a day in his riding career when he forgot to weigh in and still got away with it. John never hit the big time as a jockey and spent a lot of time riding bad horses. One day at Uttoxeter he had managed to finish third on an apparent no-hoper, to the effusive delight of all the connections, who kept him talking for an age in the unsaddling enclosure. When he finally prised himself away from the throng, John went up the weighing-room steps and turned directly left into the jockeys' room. It was only then that he remembered he should have weighed in and, technically, he was past the point of no return. With great presence of mind, John kept walking to the very back of the weighing-room and climbed out of the window. Then he walked quickly back to the steps and came in again, sitting on the scales with, no doubt, an aggrieved aside to the clerk about the time it had taken his owners to dissect the race.

Mention of Uttoxeter brings me to racecourse facilities. This course is run by the entrepreneurial Stan Clarke, who has achieved marvels in a relatively short space of time, upgrading all the facilities and attracting decent prize money, good fields and outstanding crowds. This is an outstanding example of a track coming into the 1990s, but many more deserve praise, too. When I started, there were plenty of courses where the jockeys' accommodation comprised a wooden shack with one basin and one toilet. We have moved on, almost everywhere, from such primitive times, and even Fakenham, which remains a monument to another age, has overcome some of the discomfort of the weighing-room by putting vinyl on the ceiling to stop the incessant drips of condensation!

Racing is, I believe, getting its act together, albeit slowly. It still needs more go-ahead characters, it needs better and stronger marketing, and it needs an injection of capital to bring the meagre prize money up to date and halt the exodus of owners. I realise we have been suffering a recession, hitting every industry in the country, but like everyone else in racing I believe the government has done shamefully little for what is not just a sport but a massive source of employment. We are racing for less prize money than was available five or six years ago, and that has to be a crazy situation. Last year I rode in novice hurdles worth £700 to the winner. For the owner, this would barely be enough to cover his expenses, while the jockey finds himself in the absurd position of earning more from his £74 riding fee than from his £70 cut if he actually wins the race.

'Well, Joel, the only way you'll get a ride is if they start elephant racing!' With Joel Garner, the West Indies fast bowler.

'Well, boss, it's like this . . .' With Mark Tompkins.

Receiving a prize from Lady Vestey.

156

Discussing the finer
points with Senior
Handicapper
Christopher
Mordaunt.

Talking to the late
John Paul, who will
always be remembered.

Modelling raincoats with Peter Scudamore.

The art of riding short!

Chapter Thirteen

R acing has given me a lifestyle many would envy. Work hard,
play hard, has always been my motto, and I make certain I
take my share of holidays. A week's skiing in midwinter and a
summer fortnight in Portugal with Francome is about my ideal.
In the summer of 1992, however, I did something completely
different. No sun and sand, just a working week in Russia,
climaxing in one of the most memorably mad races of my career.

Riding in Russia was a niggling ambition of mine. Having
travelled almost all the steeplechasing world, this was an elusive
final frontier and so, when the offer came to make up a British
quartet with Carl Llewellyn, Luke Harvey and Marcus Armytage,
I had no hesitation in cancelling all other plans and packing my
bags.

It was an eye-opener of a trip which I would not have missed
for the world. Equally, I have no burning desire to go there
again. The abiding memory of Russia I brought home with me
can be summed up in one word: poverty. Never again, I vowed,
will I complain about Britain's recessions, about the bills on the
mat and the occasional need for belt-tightening. Compared with
the economic plight of the Russians, we British don't know we
are born.

The point was quickly brought home to us, and in a most
appropriate way. Our plane landed in Moscow and, for a couple
of nights, we were put up at a hotel next to the Hippodrome
where, until recently, both horseracing and trotting was staged.
Only trotting survives, for the poignant reason that the authorities
could no longer afford to feed all the horses. The racehorses

might only run once a month but the trotters can be turned out every week; they stayed in work on grounds of productivity. No one told us what had happened to the racehorses.

Moscow held no appeal for me. Even the history of the place seemed to be depressed and bankrupt. Corruption was rife, money-changers on every street corner, and the snaking queues leading out of every basic food shop were pitiful to witness. The people we dealt with were friendly, and managed to remain indomitably cheerful. I often wondered how.

We were to ride in a town called Pietadorsk and, on arrival at the racecourse, it was quickly obvious that this was no Sandown Park. The grass was almost knee-high around the track but the fences, we thought, did not look too intimidating, mostly being flimsy hedges with a few ditches thrown in. Our translator smiled ominously at our confidence, however, and revealed the sort of surprise we could have done without. The locals had reasoned that the course needed spicing up to give us British jockeys a more realistic test, so they had built a new fence. It was a brick wall, three feet high, with a thick tree trunk across the top, the whole thing painted white to lend an unattractively eerie effect.

What we were not told at that time, however, was that the obstacle was so new that none of the horses due to take part in our races had ever jumped it before. This, it turned out, was a rather significant omission.

The competition was scheduled over three races and, on looking up the form of my first ride, I was happy enough. He had jumped round the course twice (though not, as I was to discover, the whole course) and finished respectably. I set out in hope, an emotion which failed to last until the race had begun, let alone ended.

It is the custom on European racetracks for the runners to jump a practice fence on the way to the start. It can be quite a decent idea to get the horse's eye in, but I can tell you it wrecks a jockey's confidence when his horse, one might say, forgets his lines in rehearsal. Mine made such a mess of the practice jump that I was lucky to stay on board, and it was a chastened Smith Eccles who joined the other runners at the start.

My instructions, according to the interpreter, were to put the horse in the race from the off, sitting handily in second or third place. Discretion was by now a much stronger suit than valour in my thoughts however, and I decided to ignore all that, feigning a misunderstanding, and drop my horse out the back.

The job, in fact, was done for me. We seemed to have been milling around at the start for an absolute age and, when we asked why, we were surprised to learn that races in Russia are not allowed off until everyone in the crowd has finished betting. We were still digesting this unusual custom when a trumpet sounded from the stands and the starter promptly called across to us to make a line. In Britain, starters are meticulous, and the runners in a jump race will invariably remain under orders until every horse is up close to the tapes, pointing in the right direction and plainly ready to set off. Not so, apparently, in Russia. Luke Harvey and I were still pulling down our goggles and turning our horses to face the start, when we realised he had let us go and the leaders were already making their way towards the first fence.

This suited me well enough, as it turned out, and I was happy to bring up the rear as the field of twelve ploughed through the long grass. We were soon reduced by three, but all four Brits were among the nine left standing as we approached the new fence. I had now moved up stealthily into fourth place and felt I was going well, tracking the short-odds favourite under Carl Llewellyn.

Now, I have ridden around Aintree plenty of times and seen all manner of falls, but never in my life have I seen such carnage at a fence as now took place. Nine went into the white-painted brick wall but only two came out. The most remarkable thing was that none were brought down. All seven fell independently, simply unable to cope with the fence the like of which they had never previously encountered.

They were not soft falls, either. They were purlers. My horse crashed into the top of the fence, shooting me out the other side, and by the time I finished rolling I was fully fifty yards further on. I lay for a moment, curled instinctively into a ball, then counted and flexed my vital limbs and discovered with some surprise that everything was still in working order. Lifting my head to survey the battlefield scene at the fence, I realised I was the lucky one.

All three of my team-mates were lying prostrate, none of them looking in imminent danger of getting to their feet. I jumped up, yelling cheery abuse at them, and found that this was, indeed, the case. Carl had broken ribs, Luke had broken his collarbone and Marcus had damaged knee ligaments. Midway through the first race, I was the only one of the British team left standing. There was no choice but to abandon the competition.

Technically, I was fit enough to have ridden again, but I politely declined all offers. Flying the flag for Britain is dear to my heart, but me against the rest of Russia – and that confounded brick wall – seemed an unfair contest. There was, in addition, no mercenary lure to it. We had been told that our riding fee, for each race in which we took part, was 500 rubles. This sounds a lot and, when the notes were handed over, it certainly felt like a respectable wad. Further enquiries, however, revealed that at the existing exchange rate we could expect a return of about £3.50. Not worth breaking bones for, international spirit or not.

If the racing was over for us, there was still plenty to enjoy during the rest of the week. The Russians were overwhelmingly hospitable, but it came in a curious mix with their naturally stiff formality. So, each evening, at whichever reception or dinner we found ourselves being feted, the routine was always the same. Copious amounts of vodka would appear and every Russian official in turn would stand up and make a toast. As each toast required us to throw back a shot of neat vodka in one, and as this drink, unfamiliar to my palate, tasted something like aviation fuel, I found the constant round of toasts having an unusual effect on me. The first would numb the back of my throat and the second would numb my brain. By the time I had downed a third and probably a fourth, I was all for getting to my feet and slurring out some toast of my own to keep the party going. By no stretch of the imagination could messrs Llewellyn, Harvey, Armytage and Smith Eccles be thought the most successful sporting team to represent Britain overseas. Taken over the course of the week, however, we may well have been the least sober.

Travelling has always been in me. I may have been brought up in a small and close community, in which a day trip to Derby was a fairly major outing, but I never did lack the spirit of adventure and, given the chance to explore, I spread my wings happily.

It was a man named Peter Thompson who encouraged me to go to America for the first time. I was twenty-five and, although a married man, I had no scruples about going on what Peter euphemistically described as a working holiday. John Burke, a great riding mate of mine, was my travelling companion for six weeks I am never likely to forget.

Peter is as American as they come but he is also a very familiar face on British racecourses. He has had horses in training here for many years, first with Tim Forster, then John Webber and latterly Simon Sherwood. He always goes for big, staying chasers and he has had his share of decent winners. Back in the mists of time, around 1980, his pride and joy was a horse called Medoc. Captain Forster trained him and I was his usual jockey. He had been in great form that winter and Peter, following his usual dedicated, if eccentric, pattern of flying across the Atlantic each time he had a runner in England, was mighty pleased. So pleased, indeed, that he offered to pay my passage to the States in the close-season. It took no persuasion for him to count John Burke in, too, although I was wondering about the wisdom of this when Burkey's Irish passport caused us an interminable delay in immigration at Washington airport.

Peter is an influential guy, though, and, with the suspicions allayed we were sent on our way. The typical American limo, economy no consideration, in which Peter had driven to the airport, was waiting to take us to the Thompson home in America's lush green jump-racing country, Maryland. But it was a long drive, Peter was weary and so the wheel was handed over to yours truly. Feeling like a swank yank, I covered the miles at a good gallop but, cruising through some suburban town and dicing with the amber at traffic lights, I was suddenly aware of a clamour of sirens and flashing blue lights. The state police had a victim and, tempting though it was to indulge in one of those spine-chilling car chases from the American cop series on TV, I pulled over obediently and, trained in such matters back home, sprang out of the car to try and charm the duty officer.

Peter might have told me that this was not the done thing in the States. But Peter, like Burkey in the back, was fast asleep. I was all alone and my confidence in handling what was not an unfamiliar scenario to me shrank alarmingly as one of the cops produced a gun while the other roughly spun me round and spread me across the side of Peter's car, arms thrust above my head.

Life did not seem quite so worth living at that moment but, dumb with panic, it occurred to me I might not have to suffer it much longer. That gun was poised very menacingly. Were all the stories about American police really true? Was I about to find out and become just another statistic?

I have always been very fond of Peter Thompson but never been as grateful to hear his distinctive voice as I was now. Roused from his slumbers by the activity, he unpeeled himself from the passenger seat and set about explaining to the confrontational types in uniform that I was not a criminal on the run but a poor, innocent limey who knew no better. They needed a bit of convincing but, at length, the gun was re-holstered and I was allowed to resume a more dignified standing position, feeling as I did so that the welcome I had so far received from the guardians of the United States fell short of cordiality. Things could only improve, and so they did, though not before I had another unnerving experience. We stayed a week in Peter's palatial mansion but I spent only one night in the room I was initially given. I am not an impressionable type and had always scoffed at the very possibility of ghosts, but I swear that room was haunted. I hardly slept the first night; on the second, I experienced a dramatic drop in temperature and the quite unmistakable touch of a hand on my leg. Yes, I was alone. Yes, I was sober. Yes, I scuttled out of that room so fast my feet hardly touched the ground and, for the rest of the stay I shared a twin room with Burkey. My convictions over what had happened were in no way shaken when the housemaid later told us of a tale that, years before, a young boy had died of appendicitis in that very room.

The working part of the trip began in earnest after we hitched a lift from Belmont Park, the New York racecourse, up to Saratoga. The horsebox in which we travelled through the night was not the most comfortable conveyance and, stiff and unshaven, I felt I was back in the grip of ghosts when we arrived in the early half-light of morning and the first person I saw, riding work on the course, was our friend and colleague Richard Linley.

This was a stroke of good fortune in more ways than one, because Richard was living in a flat, conveniently near to the Saratoga course, and we were able to move into the same block. Richard showed us the ropes, and the local sights, and for the next fortnight we had a tremendous time if you disregard the working hours, which required a 4 a.m. start in total darkness and a begging-bowl round of the training barns seeking some work-riding from surly and suspicious head lads. The money was handy when it came but after a few days of this unsociable routine, I settled on spending my own cash and having a holiday.

Three years later I returned to America, and to Maryland, but this time as a proud member of the first Great Britain jump jockeys' team. This was a private enterprise, indeed the brainchild of my co-author, but it met with the unanimous approval of the jockeys. Ours is an individual sport but so, too, are tennis, golf and athletics. They all have team events, where the leading players can feel they are representing their country, so why not us? The concept was sound, from our viewpoint, because it is acknowledged around the world that British jump jockeys are the best because they have the most practice. Ours is the only full-time professional circuit in the world; so our leading jockeys are appreciated world-wide, something we were to find out during a few eventful years of foreign trips.

Peter Thompson played his part in helping to organise the debut 'away match' for the team. It was to be on his local track at Fair Hill, which later became the venue for the Breeders Cup steeplechase in which I also rode more than once. Four international races were built into the card for a Saturday meeting in early June, immediately after the end of our domestic season, and there were to be teams of four jockeys each from America and Britain, with mounts decided by ballot.

I don't know of a single jockey who would not have jumped at the chance of riding for his country on a trip like this, but only four could go and John Francome was automatically first choice. Jonjo was quickly added and, as Peter Scudamore was by now firmly established as a title challenger, he was the third pick. I won the last place just ahead of Hywel Davies, seniority winning the day! David Nicholson was our team manager.

We flew out from Gatwick, to Baltimore, on the Thursday morning, arriving in good time to view the course and attend the draw for rides. Our accommodation was provided by local trainers and it was not of the Len Carrod caravan-in-field variety. I stayed with Burley Cocks, a grand old chap who has been among the leading US jumping trainers for many years, but, what with one thing and another, I saw very little of my appointed billet. The Americans did not stint when it came to entertaining us and a marquee reception on the Friday night filtered inconveniently into Saturday morning. I awoke, I knew not where or with whom, feeling pretty dehydrated, and one peep at the weather outside assured me that this condition was likely to be incurable. Breakfast-time, and already it was into the mid-eighties. By the time I linked up with the other boys at the course the thermometer was nudging the century, a mark it comfortably exceeded in the course of the afternoon. Fair Hill is a good course to ride round but its facilities, at the time, were not quite up to Ascot standard and, in the cramped confines of the weighing-room our recurring cry, through the meeting, was for water and ice. Franc collapsed after his third ride but came round in time to win on his last, the result which decided the first transatlantic jumping match in favour of the Brits.

There was nothing for it but to celebrate and we did a pretty good job at that, too. Saturday evening was spent in the splendour of Mrs Miles Valentine's house. Mrs Valentine, whose pink and purple colours are well known on British courses through her patronage for many years of Fred Winter's yard, wanted to put on a party for us, largely because Franc had ridden her so many winners. It was a memorable night, and when another trainer staged a Sunday lunchtime binge on our behalf, we were left with a mad dash up the freeway to catch our early-evening flight home. This time, thankfully, there were no interventions from gun-toting cops.

If that was a memorable trip, it was capped several times over the following June, when the team embarked on a tour so ambitious it seemed sure to attract disaster. In the space of three weeks, we went around the world, making a return visit to Maryland before a match against Australia spanning several meetings in Victoria, and finally a similar competition in New Zealand. Franc had retired and Scu had taken over as captain, with me as his lieutenant and chief agitator. John Williams, clerk of the course at Hereford, took the role of team manager and proved what a sound, unflappable character he is.

It would be wrong to say this was an entirely untroubled trip. We could hardly expect that it would be. We were venturing into uncharted waters and there were sure to be hitches. New Zealand provided the majority of these, for the travel arrangements fell down, the local welcome initially seemed ungenuine and one of the country courses we rode on was, frankly, so dangerous it would not have been operating in Britain. I lost my temper now and again, even threatened to fly home, one day in Auckland. That is me. But my enduring memories of the tour are all good ones.

We beat the Americans again, the day before my thirtieth birthday. I celebrated in style and was thrown, fully clothed, into our hotel swimming pool. Then it was on, via Los Angeles, to Melbourne, and to hospitality which even put the Americans in the shade. We were big news in Australia. The media had latched onto the contest and every member of the team found himself being interviewed by the newspapers or featured on TV news programmes. One interview I undertook, for an Adelaide radio station, has become a well-chronicled classic of weighing-room banter; I was productively engaged in my hotel room with a local Australian lass, at the time.

I have never been pampered as we were in Melbourne, never felt such a celebrity as when I rode two televised winners on a big card at Moonee Valley, one of Melbourne's plush metro-politan tracks. It spoiled me, of course, and New Zealand came as a bit of a downer. The weather was appalling, the racing not much better, and the accommodation was decidedly moderate. By then, however, I was fully adjusted to hotel life and relishing the independence of it all to such an extent that I found it difficult to re-adapt to home life when, at last, we returned.

There was no welcoming crowd at the airport, no TV crews to record the homecoming heroes. Most people in Britain, even racing folk I think, were unaware of where we had been, or why. But as a team we felt a sense of pride and achievement. We had crossed a few barriers in the course of that hectic three weeks and, by and large, I think we had been good representatives of our country. Our smart team uniform, blazer, slacks and tie for functions and travelling, black anoraks with Great Britain badge for racing, had been admired everywhere and, undoubtedly, had made us feel a unit rather than a few jockeys on a beano. We felt we had done something worthwhile, not just for ourselves but for British racing as a whole.

The national team trips went on for a few good years, though never again on such a grand scale. We had an annual match against Belgium, usually in Ostend but once in Brussels, and we went twice to France. The second such trip was part of a novel, three-sided international, also involving the Irish, who staged their home leg in Galway.

Over the years I have ridden on a lot of Irish courses and drunk a lot of Irish whisky. I have met plenty of wild and wonderful Irish characters and, each time I go back, I fall in love with the place all over again. It was a trip to Ireland which rescued the 1991–92 season for me, when I had all but written it off as one of the most miserable of my career.

The Ballinrostig affair had soured the season early on; the broken ankle had ruined it. Watching Cheltenham, rather than riding, was torture and although I was fit enough to resume at Aintree, I did not ride a winner. The closest I came was on Mark Tompkins' Staunch Friend, who had been sent off favourite for the Triumph Hurdle at Cheltenham but, puzzlingly, had run no sort of race and been pulled up by Adrian Maguire before jumping the last.

Sent to Aintree to try and redeem his reputation, he partially succeeded, but in finishing second, three-and-a-half lengths behind a horse who finished fifth in the Triumph, he had still not produced his best. Four weeks later, at the Punchestown festival, he did so in the most devastating style.

It was a high-class field for the Guinness Champion four-year-old race, and so it should have been with almost £30,000 on offer to the winner. Duke of Monmouth, who won the Triumph, was running, along with Salwan, who had beaten us at Aintree, and Muir Station, still a maiden but considered by the Irish to be 'the business' and, ridden by Scu, duly sent off favourite.

In the heavy ground that day, it was a no contest. I knew this was a good horse but I had no idea how good until, having tracked Muir Station and Duke of Monmouth, I sent him about his business between the last two hurdles. Staunch Friend found another gear and, as the others began to flounder in the mud, he quickened away from them as if they were selling-platers at Plumpton rather than the best of the juveniles from either side of the Irish Sea.

Staunch Friend won by twelve lengths, a margin I could almost have doubled if necessary. The season had its highlight, after all, and although my thirty-seventh birthday was beckoning, and Sir Piers Bengough might think my boots needed hanging up, I had plenty to look forward to when the new season began in August. They were not getting rid of me just yet.

Chapter Fourteen

Twelve months on, the crossroads confronted me more starkly than ever before. There was no getting away from it, the season had been disappointing and, at times, even disenchanting. Thirty winners was not a lot to show, by my career-long standards, for ten months of slog in which I had lost, as a colleague, my friend and weighing-room neighbour when Peter Scudamore retired, and lost many of my best rides when Mark Tompkins very publicly sacked me.

Once into May, the season can never end soon enough for me. It has always been the same. But as spring became summer in 1993, I was feeling more than just the usual fatigue and need of a holiday. I was at an age when most of my peers had hung up their boots and, it seemed, I was widely expected to do the same. But I didn't want to; I wasn't ready. If, at the crossroads where I found myself, the road straight ahead was distinctly narrow, those to either side were not even signposted.

There are things I want to do when I give up riding, and most of them are connected with racing. After more than twenty years in the game it would be madness to think otherwise. The expansion of televised racing interests me and, as someone who is reasonably knowledgeable and articulate, I like to think I might have a future in that direction. There are other offshoots, too, such as overseas travel and corporate entertaining, which may occupy me increasingly. But as the 1992–93 season proceeded, my overriding emotion was not at all the desire to retire but a resentment that people were making that assumption of me.

It was not as if I had lost my bottle. In the upper-thirties age bracket only the incurably mad will ride a novice chaser who cannot jump with the same devil-may-care spirit which infects the lower-twenties. In this respect, age brings wisdom, and a desire to live a little longer. But put me on a horse with a genuine winning chance and, senior rider or not, I still believe I have the edge, tactically, technically and physically, on most of the new generation. Just ask anyone who saw me win on Sibton Abbey at Cheltenham's January meeting, one of my few big winners of the season and a ride which came my way only through a comical misunderstanding.

Jockeys need, as much as anything, to be mobile and available, so my situation this past season was not helped by a run-in with the Essex police on the M11. I was narrowly over the limit, both in speed and alcohol terms, and as one caution followed another, I knew that a difficult year inevitably awaited me. The customary twelve-month ban was duly enforced and I spent the season begging lifts. It was a novel experience, being driven everywhere, and I relied heavily on the goodwill of friends and neighbours in Newmarket to ferry me about. It was not quite the logistical nightmare it might have been, though, and it certainly kept me alert.

On the Saturday in question, I had been driven down to Cheltenham by another jockey and was due for just the one ride, on James Fanshawe's useful juvenile, Storm Dust. I knew I had to find a lift back, however, and my eyes lit up when Ferdy Murphy came into the weighing-room, where I was having my usual mid-afternoon tea and sandwich. Ferdy is the retained trainer of that wealthy owner, Geoff Hubbard, at his stables in Suffolk, not too far from Newmarket. Without bothering to wonder what he was doing in the weighing-room with a worried frown on his face, I hailed him noisily and got up from my seat. Ferdy's gaze had been scanning the room but now, reacting to my yell, he glanced at me and nodded. 'OK, Ecc, you can ride him,' he said.

I was not exactly half asleep. My mind had been plenty active enough that afternoon, but occupied almost exclusively with the problem of getting myself back somewhere near base that evening. I had been peripherally aware that Declan Murphy had been injured during an incident-packed hurdle race, but had not taken that to its logical conclusion, which was that Ferdy (no relation) now required a jockey for the highly promising handicap chaser, Sibton Abbey. Quite by accident, I had volunteered myself for the ride, and secured it. If I say so myself, I proceeded to give one of my better performances. I would go so far as to say that the horse would not have won with too many others on board.

Sibton Abbey was having a very good season and had already won the Hennessy, ridden by Adrian Maguire. The Gold Cup at Cheltenham was the next obvious target and, as Maguire was booked for Cool Ground, on whom he had won the race twelve months earlier, I kept the ride on Sibton Abbey. He gave a good account, too, finishing fifth, and I was so impressed that I told the press he would win it next year. I hoped, having made his acquaintance in somewhat muddled circumstances, that I would still be on top when he proved me right.

Falling into a top-class ride like this was the exception to the season's rule, for me. Rides of any kind, indeed, became ever more scarce as the spring arrived. I was stranded on thirty winners for what seemed an endless number of weeks, but my racecourse appearances in that time were rare. There were two reasons for this, the first being an almost total absence of 'spare' rides with stables for whom I do not regularly work.

I still, technically, had Ian Wardle as my agent, and we remained on very friendly terms. But agents and me simply were not made for each other. Ian might have worked his socks off on the phone for a few hours before calling to tell me he had got me on a novice chaser at Bangor. In all probability, I would tell him to forget it. Call me ungrateful, call me irresponsible, the fact is I did not want the hassle of having to negotiate a six-hour journey, without my own car, for the dubious privilege of trying to steer a dodgy jumper round a country track.

I know that Adrian Maguire would have taken the ride, or Richard Dunwoody even. I know that is why Dunwoody is now champion, why Maguire almost certainly will be and why I never was. But we are all made differently. Rightly or wrongly, I believed that I had been around long enough for trainers to know what I could offer. I did not necessarily expect them to come running to me offering good rides but it disillusioned me quite badly when I did phone up for a spare ride and got a knockback, invariably in favour of some kid I know very well I could ride the backside off. It could be a sign of age, but I found it increasingly undignified to be scratching around for the cast-offs.

The second reason for my declining season related to the two trainers I had imagined would give me a steady supply of winners, Tompkins in Newmarket and Tim Thomson Jones in Lambourn. For contrasting reasons, neither came up to expectations.

In some ways, Mark Tompkins and I were made for each other, a working relationship between two men of like mind. In another way, what happened between us was close to inevitable, for we are two pieces of flint. When they rub together, sparks will fly.

Like so many partings, ours came through something relatively trivial which might, with cooler heads on both sides, have been easily resolved. That it was not, that it caused headlines and then festered unhealthily through the remainder of the season, said something about our respective personalities.

It was the end of February, the time which, in his mitigation, could be called Mark's most stressful of the year. He is very much a dual-purpose trainer, his thirty-odd jumpers augmenting a flat-race team of maybe twice that number, and, as the climax of the National Hunt season approaches, he also has to contend with priming his younger horses for the imminent start of the flat campaign. If this was his excuse for what happened, mine was that I was poleaxed by flu. As someone who very seldom gets ill, I resented this as an intrusion and an inconvenience, more than a discomfort. Its first effect on the business side of things was when I had to get off a ready-made winner for Mark, which did not please either of us.

Highbrook, a winning mare on the flat and owned by the England and Northamptonshire cricketer, Nick Cook, was due to make her hurdling debut at Catterick on the Thursday of that week. I was looking forward to riding her. But I took to my bed, reluctantly but quite unavoidably, on the Wednesday and, the following morning, it was obvious to me that I would be doing neither myself nor the horse and her connections any favours by trying to ride her. I was as weak as a kitten and, although I did not envisage her requiring very much help from the saddle to win, it was no state in which to even attempt riding.

I phoned Mark and told him the problem, adding that I thought my old granny could win on her, let alone Ross Campbell, who does most of the work-riding for the yard and is a capable young pilot. I told him I expected to be fit again by the weekend and, as he had entries at both Kempton and Haydock, asked him where he would like me to go. Mark, though, was now in a thoroughly bad temper and all he offered by way of reply was a barked: 'Go where you want,' before the phone was put down with a crash.

Later that day, feeling slightly better in myself if a shade cross that I had, as expected, missed an easy winner at Catterick, I went back to the telephone and checked on Tim Thomson Jones' Saturday plans. He did not have much to run apart from a hurdler whose owners were keen that I should ride him. As Mark had effectively, if testily, given me a free hand, I agreed to go to Kempton, where I felt the Tompkins horse, Eden's Close, had a good chance in the Tote Placepot Hurdle for four-year-olds.

Next morning, Mark was back on the phone, initially in better humour. It did not last. He now wanted me to go to Haydock to ride another of his four-year-olds, Glaisdale. He had run only once over hurdles, beating a highly regarded horse of Josh Gifford's at Towcester, and was plainly a possible for the Triumph Hurdle at Cheltenham. I did not think the ground at Haydock would be as soft as he would like it but this reservation had nothing to do with my plans. The fact was, I now felt committed to going to Kempton, but here was Mark trying to insist I should go elsewhere. I made a token effort, phoning Tim again to check, but received the expected and understandable response that his owners would not take kindly to me getting off their horse having already agreed to ride it. There was nothing more I could do. I rang Mark back to tell him and he blew his top completely.

His last words were, from memory: 'If you don't go to Haydock, that's it between us.' Dramatic, maybe, but although we had fallen out, I considered Mark a good friend as well as a good employer and felt sure that it would all blow over. I knew differently on Saturday morning, when I opened my *Sporting Life* and scanned the opposition in the Placepot Hurdle. The first thing to strike me was that I was no longer involved in the race: R. Campbell appeared in the jockeys' column next to Eden's Close.

Reasoning that it was best not to provoke a further argument, I said nothing, rode Tim's horse and went home again. I didn't even see Mark at the races – he may well have been at Haydock – and we had still not spoken when my mobile phone rang on the following Tuesday. It was a news reporter from the *Sporting Life*, wanting a comment from me on being jocked off Staunch Friend in the Champion Hurdle. As I knew nothing about it, and could not bring myself to believe it, I had nothing to say. All too soon, though, the truth of it became apparent. Mark was quoted in the next morning's *Life*, putting me in a pretty poor light, and he barely left the door ajar for us ever to work together again. Adrian Maguire was to replace me on Staunch Friend; he would, said Mark, find the best available to ride the rest of the stable's jumpers.

Fast ground at Cheltenham utterly ruined Staunch Friend's prospects in the Champion, but he did later go to Scotland and win the equivalent race there. This, in fact, was a rare high point as Mark ended the season pretty quietly, but I took small consolation from that. I had lost a very good job, through what I maintain was no fault of my own.

An olive branch, of sorts, was offered one morning in May when Mark jumped out of his car on spotting me riding out in Gavin Pritchard-Gordon's string. He invited me round for a cup of tea and I was there half-an-hour later, the two of us chatting away, as friendly as ever. Typically, between two proud and stubborn characters, the upset was not even mentioned but, the following morning, I was once again riding out for Tompkins, and continued to do so through the summer. It remains to be seen if business will resume as before but, naturally, I hope so.

The Thomson Jones yard had looked all set for a successful season and, as I had the agreement to ride the pick of the horses, I expected this to provide me with a regular supply of winners. I was especially looking forward to being reunited with Keep Talking and Norman Conqueror, still in the yard despite the death of their grand old owner, Jim Joel. In his will, he had requested that the Queen Mother should have her pick of his steeplechasers; wisely, it seemed, she chose Keep Talking as her 'gift horse', but also took on two others in the yard, Norman Conqueror and Skinnhill. All three could have been expected to win but I had to wait until late March, and a bad race at Wolverhampton, to achieve another of my ambitions by riding a winner for the Queen Mother on Skinnhill.

Her other two horses were responsible for my major disappointments. From the start of the season, Tim and I agreed that Norman Conqueror would be ideally suited by the Aintree fences and the two miles six furlongs of the John Hughes Handicap, on the opening day of the Grand National meeting. Barely a week before the race, he developed a leg problem and was out for the rest of the season. As for Keep Talking, he ran well once in defeat, at Newbury's New Year meeting, but was not right at any stage of the season. Like the majority of Tim's horses, he was suffering from that all-consuming racing term, 'the virus', a disorder usually indistinguishable until a horse gets into a racing situation, when he will simply be unable to produce his true running.

Tim's was not the only yard in Lambourn to be affected but it certainly seemed to hang around his stable longer than any of the others. The virus demoralises everyone within a yard, so completely does it destroy the reason for racing, and, although I was suffering its consequences, I felt more sorry for Tim and his staff than I did for myself.

There had been some thought, early in the season, of aiming Keep Talking at the Grand National. Considering he was only a year out of novice status, it will have done him no harm to wait for another season to tackle Aintree – another good reason for continuing to ride – but with no attractive alternatives presenting themselves, I was without a ride in the National. Good thing, as it turned out. I was able to sit in the weighing-room, quite dispassionately, and observe the greatest cock-up in racing history at close quarters.

The story must be familiar to almost everyone in the country. You would certainly have needed to spend the day of the race, and several which followed, deep in a bunker, cut off from all communications, to be unaware of the most dramatic story even this race has ever produced. There was, of course, no race – at least, none which counted for anything. After two false starts, however, enough of the field continued for a full circuit to render a third try impracticable and a handful ploughed on for the second circuit, too. I have to say that I could not understand them.

Given the adrenalin which flows at the start of the National, and the woefully inadequate procedures for recalling jockeys after a false start, it was no surprise that some completed a circuit. But as they approached The Chair, right in front of a booing, catcalling main stand, there were enough bollards in front of the fence for them to be aware of the situation, and enough people and horses milling around at the start, directly ahead of them, to have no doubts that they should stop.

I happen to know there was a conversation between two of those who went on, as they approached Bechers for the second time. Both were Irish jockeys, I have to say, and one said: 'I think we should pull up now, something is obviously wrong.' The other replied: 'Bugger that, I'm going too well.'

I felt a certain sympathy for John White, who 'won' the race-which-never-was on Jenny Pitman's Esha Ness, but his body language on the run-in, and as he passed the post, said everything necessary. He knew very well the race was void.

Back in the weighing-room, war had broken out in earnest. Trainers, owners, stewards and jockeys were all shouting at once, nobody making much sense and everyone getting angrier by the moment. I don't think I have ever seen such an emotional scene and, as the full consequences of what had taken place were assessed, the damage to racing's image and finances was grimly detailed.

Hindsight may prove that a lot of good came out of the shambles, so long as the various enquiries impress upon the Jockey Club that, all too often, racing presents itself as an accident waiting to happen. We have a marvellous sport, the most competitive in the world, yet it has been run, at the highest level, by complacent men when what is needed are men of vision, who will improve the game before mistakes are made, not react to them when they are.

A series of minor incidents, set off by the Animal Rights demonstration a furlong down the course and compounded by the first false start, conspired to produce the National's day of chaos. But, even in the heat of difficult moments, there were things which could and should have been done to avoid the ultimate embarrassment; those in authority were simply not thinking on their feet. The only thing those in racing could be thankful about was that, on their blackest day, nobody died, nobody was even injured. It was not a Hillsborough, with its death and devastating consequences, it was just a day on which the uncommitted laughed their heads off at the ineptitude of those running horse-racing.

It was a particularly bad season for the Jockey Club, their handling of another doping scandal causing some justifiable condemnation, and to men such as myself, the evidence was now overwhelming for the old guard to move over and make way for people with the knowledge that can only come from shop-floor involvement in the sport over many years.

Similar views to these were expressed by Peter Scudamore after the National and it was no surprise to me when he retired the following Wednesday. I do not believe it was the National itself which dictated his timing, although his greatest remaining ambition had been dashed by the non-event. I just feel he knew the time was right, knew he could no longer motivate himself in the formidably dedicated style which had made him the great and enduring champion he was. Cross-country drives from Hereford to Market Rasen on Saturdays in late May must eventually lose their appeal when you have achieved as much as Scu and he did not have the old, burning desire to chase Richard Dunwoody in the championship race. And so, typically, he stage-managed the whole thing, right down to riding a winner, at Ascot, on his final ride. It could not have been scripted any better and I know of nobody in racing who would begrudge him one word of the many accolades which came his way.

In a way, I was surprised Pete had ridden for as long as he did. Two years earlier, I was with him in the ambulance room at Market Rasen after a fall from Charlie Brooks' hurdler, Black Humour, had broken his leg. The truth may come out when defences are down and Scu, in great pain, left me in no doubt that he was teetering on the brink. I know he thought about retiring in the days which followed; I am also convinced that one more bad fall would have decided him. I am glad for him that it did not happen in that fashion, and that he was able to go out on a day, and in a way, that he could not have hand-chosen any better.

That the decision was right is evident in Scu now. He doesn't miss riding at all, and he has begun to look far more human than the haggard, pasty-faced figure with bags under the eyes who sat next to me, day after day, for several seasons. As a jockey, Scu was a workaholic. He may be the same in other spheres now, and I am sure he will make a success of whatever he does, because he is that type of guy. But for one who was not a natural in the saddle, he made himself the complete race-rider by endless work and attention to detail, and he established a partnership with Martin Pipe which revolutionised jump racing.

I have been with him when he has spent, literally, hours on a phone call to Pipe. I couldn't have done it. Similarly, I have seen, all too clearly, the way he pushed himself in search of perfection, be it on the racecourse itself or in starving himself for days on end to make a particularly light weight.

Scu is a very good friend and, close as we are, it has naturally occurred to me to wonder why I couldn't be more like him and whether, if I had been, the champion's title might have come my way even once. Although Scu cannot match my three Champion Hurdles, I have not had anything like his success. However, I suspect that every now and again he looked at me with a shade of envy because, by God, I have enjoyed myself!

I admit there have been times, when the going has been rough and tough, that I have been tempted to hang up my boots but because I cannot think of any job that could possibly give me so much pleasure, I do not intend to vacate the number one peg in the weighing room just yet.

After all, another See You Then might be round the next corner.

Index

181